DEFAULT!

DEFAULT!

John Charles Pool

Ross M. LaRoe
Denison University

St. Martin's Press   New York

Library of Congress Catalog Card Number: 87-060562
Copyright © 1988 by St. Martin's Press, Inc.
All Rights Reserved.
Manufactured in the United States of America.
21098
fedcba
For information, write:
St. Martin's Press, Inc.
175 Fifth Avenue
New York, NY 10010

cover design: Darby Downey

ISBN: 0-312-00518-0

To Our Parents

Preface

We wrote this book out of a serious conviction that the international financial system is heading toward a crisis that may have serious consequences for us all.

The international financial system purports to facilitate the exchange of goods and services between countries and, in the process, raise each citizen's well-being. As countries specialize in what they do best and trade in their respective products, international trade is supposed to provide higher standards of living and higher incomes. Indeed, historically the system has performed well, albeit with varying degrees of success and not a little controversy.

But nowadays the story of international economics is a story of debt. The United States has an internal debt of more than $2 trillion and a foreign debt estimated to approach $1 trillion by 1990. And the already impoverished Third World countries are indebted to the industrialized world by at least $1 trillion.

It was in the early 1970s that the system began to break down. The Arab oil embargo and the unprecedented seventeen-fold increase in oil prices stimulated one of the largest transfers of wealth in history, as hundreds of billions of dollars were sent from the petroleum-dependent industrialized world to the OPEC nations in payment for badly needed oil.

These funds were then recycled back to industrialized countries in the form of deposits in the international money-center banks. They, in turn, promptly loaned them out to the capital-poor Third World. By the mid-1980s, it was obvious to almost everyone that these loans would never be repaid and that the international finance system was in a perilous condition.

In 1982, Mexico essentially declared bankruptcy but was bailed out by the now-concerned banking system. The debt situation reached crisis proportions again in 1986 and, again, Mexico was bailed out by its creditors. In early 1987, Brazil effectively declared bankruptcy, stating that it would no longer be able to pay even the interest on its $108 billion foreign debt—the largest in the Third World.

A default by only one of the large debtor countries—such as the Mexican default fictionally depicted in this book—would probably not precipitate a worldwide financial crisis, no matter how costly it might be to the overextended banks and their shareholders. However, the Third World debt situation is much like a game of dominoes. If one falls, the precedent will be set and others will most likely follow. If that happens, the international financial system will face a crisis of unprecedented proportions. That is the subject of this book.

We've written on this topic in many different, more conventional, forums, but the novel allows one to feel, understand, and experience in a way that nonfiction books, articles, and newspaper columns do not. It allows the reader to peer into the future and speculate realistically about what could happen if the system we have come to depend on should collapse. It also allows possible solutions to be explored more imaginatively.

This book should help anyone understand the mechanics of the international financial system, both in front of and behind the scenes. It should be appropriate supplemental reading for a wide range of classes in business, economics, international studies, political science, and modern history.

Our primary goal in writing *Default!* was to make this difficult and abstract topic entertaining in an educational context. As usual, the market will judge the extent to which we have accomplished that goal.

Although the settings are mostly taken from the real world, the characters, to the best of our knowledge, are all fictional.

Acknowledgments

Books like this one are the result of a combination of experiences, education, perseverance, imagination, and luck. It is, therefore, difficult to single out any one source of inspiration.

But among those who have influenced our thinking on this subject and should be mentioned are Harry Magdoff, coeditor of *Monthly Review,* and Professor Steve Stamos, Jr., of Bucknell University.

The late John D. McDonald, perhaps more than any other writer, helped us understand that the novel can be a powerful educational tool. And novelist Martin Naparsteck was an invaluable source of editorial support.

Linda Vollmer, Debbie White, and Mary Payne Wright—masters of the art of processing words—nurtured the manuscript through countless drafts, and we appreciate their efforts.

Finally, our families, Betty, Mike, and Laura Linda; and Karen, Joe, Lee, and Bob, provided their usual support, understanding, and much appreciated relentless criticism.

J.C.P.
R.M.L.

DEFAULT!

I

On every college campus there's a time each fall when you're glad you decided to be a professor instead of a banker or something like that where you make money. It comes just after Labor Day when the students come back to campus, in their cars overloaded with clothes, books, stereo systems, and these days with their own personal computers.

The freshmen come with their parents, usually dragging a U-Haul filled with new clothes they will soon find out they don't need. They're part of a seemingly neverending hoard of eighteen-year-olds who look younger every year. But they're not. I'm older, I had finally realized.

Frisbee games spring up on the still green grass of the quadrangle. There's a feeling of energy and excitement. Football is in the air. And as autumn sets in, a nip in the breeze. It's sweater time.

So I felt good on that September day. Rested from a summer at the North Shore; the latest book finished. My office was in shambles as usual, and a pile of junk mail, accumulated all summer, beckoned. I opened it methodically and piece by piece threw it into the now overflowing wastebasket. I was almost to the bottom of the pile when the phone rang. I hoped I could finish before Dan Meyers—the local police chief—got here. He had called earlier and wanted to see me about "a matter of some urgency," he had said. So I guess the mail will have to wait. The call, I imagined, was Mrs. Lincoln telling me he was here.

So I was surprised when she said, "It's the White House. The president wants to speak with you."

"Okay, thanks, Helen." I had met President Dawson when he was governor and I had chaired the state budget reduction task force. Later, when he was running for president, I wrote most of his economic policy speeches and he had tried to repay the debt by offering me the undersecretary of economic affairs at the Treasury. I was tempted but had declined. I preferred watching the football to being one. Now I supposed he had another job for me. I hoped not because it's hard to say no to a president, especially when they start talking about how "the country needs you."

"Hello."

"Professor Marshall?"

"Yes."

"Hold please, for the president."

Then the familiar voice. "Cameron? This is the president. How have you been?"

"Very well, sir, thank you."

"And how are Ann and Becky?"

"Just fine, sir. And how are you?"

"Well, not so good, Cameron. We've got a problem. Are you keeping up on the Mexican situation?"

My eyes dropped to the lead story in the morning *Times:*

> Unofficial sources say that the CIA is warning the Administration that political pressure on the Cordoba Administration is mounting.
>
> Mexico's external debt now exceeds $100 billion and

since the dramatic fall in oil prices there appears to be no way the country can earn sufficient foreign exchange to even service interest payments due for the coming year.

Political interests on both the right and the left are pressuring the President to declare a unilateral default, and there is increasing evidence that the PRI is losing its long-time grip on the country.

"Yes, I think so, sir. It looks like things are beginning to fall apart."

"Whatever you've heard, it's worse than that. My people tell me the Mexicans may default any day now."

"That would, indeed, be a problem, sir," I said, wondering what was coming next, although I was afraid I already knew. "If that happens before the economic summit conference, we will be in some *real* trouble." I have yet to figure out why they decided to hold it in Mexico City.

"How can I help, sir?"

"Well, Cameron, what I need is someone to help us out on this, but it can't be one of my regular people. That would be too obvious. I need someone the Mexicans trust, and that, as I'm sure you can imagine, doesn't include anyone here in Washington. Can you come to the conference?"

"Of course, sir. When do you want me to be there?"

"There's going to be a meeting at the embassy on Thursday morning that I'd like you to attend. Can you make it?"

"I'll be there, sir. Anything else?"

"Well, professor, as I'm sure you know, the more information we can bring to bear on the problem the better off we'll be. So you might want to get there early and nose around a bit. Talk to some of your friends. We'll have briefing papers to you by this evening."

"That'll be fine, sir."

"Okay, then. We'll see you soon. Oh, . . . and, uh, thanks, Cam."

"No problem, sir."

II

That, of course, was a bit of an understatement. In fact, there were two problems: Chief Meyers and getting to Mexico City tomorrow. I decided to deal with the second one first.

I buzzed Mrs. Lincoln. "Helen, see if you can get me on the first flight to Mexico City tomorrow morning. Make it a Mexican airline if you can. And make it first class . . . no, never mind the first class." I had forgotten that the Mexican airlines don't have first class. A last vestige of the revolution, I had always thought. That meant I'd be spending about three and half hours with my legs cramped up, and maybe the rest of me, too, since I'm about four inches taller and about fifteen or, probably more like thirty, pounds heavier than the hypothetical average person they have in mind when they design tourist-class seats.

I started to ask Mrs. Lincoln to make me a reservation at the María Isabel, and then thought better of it. The conference was to be there. I'd have a lot more freedom of movement if I stayed somewhere else. "See if you can get me one of those small suites at the Geneve."

"Yes, sir. And will you be returning?" She never missed a chance.

"Well, if you keep that up I may not. Just leave the return open."

"Yes, sir," she said in her ever efficient manner. "And will you be wanting the university limo to take you to the airport?"

Got me again. At some point you'd think a person would get tired of shooting at such an easy target. "Yes, thank you, Helen. And . . . Helen? Has Chief Meyers shown up yet?"

"Yes. I was just going to tell you. Should I send him in?"

"Yes, please. Thanks, Helen." So it was finally happening; I wasn't surprised. For one brief moment I wondered how the president knew. That, professor, I thought to myself, is a very stupid question.

Chief Meyers looked to be in his mid-to-late twenties, crew cut type. He was athletic looking, more like a state trooper than a small town police chief. I had seen him around town, but we had never met. And it was obvious that this wasn't a social call.

"What can I do for you, chief?" I asked, trying not to think about the Mexican fiasco.

"Well, sir, I wondered if you'd mind answering a few questions."

"Do I need my lawyer present?" I said, smiling for what turned out to be the last time that day.

"Do you know a person," he paused to consult his notebook, "named Arturo Octavio Cordes?"

"Yeah, sure. Why do you ask? What's this all about, chief?" Arturo had been a student of mine years ago when I had taught in Mexico. We kept in touch, but it had been a year or so since I'd heard from him. His last letter had come shortly after he had taken a position at the Ministry of Finance, working for José Muñoz, another former student and now one of my closest friends.

"I'm sorry to have to tell you this, sir, but he's dead. Murdered. Last night or sometime early this morning at the College Inn."

It was one of the few times in my life that I can remember being totally at a loss for words. Arturo dead? What was he doing here in Denville? Why would anyone want to kill him? What a terrible waste. And why was the local police chief asking me about it?

By the time I got my thoughts in some semblance of order I realized that the chief was watching me calmly and carefully, as if he were studying my reaction. Finally, I blurted out, "Surely, you don't think I had anything to do with it."

"No. No, of course not."

It was a relief, of sorts, to find out I wasn't a murder suspect, but I'd known that I hadn't killed Arturo all along. "So what brings you here to ask me about it?" I asked, regaining my composure.

"Well, sir, at this point, you're the only lead I have in the case. I have reason to believe that he was in town to see you. I know *what* happened. But not why it happened, or who did it. So, if you'll be kind enough to help me by answering a few questions, maybe we can figure it out."

"Of course. Anything I can do to help," I said. "But perhaps, first, before you do that, you could tell me exactly what happened?"

"Sure," he said. Then he consulted his notebook again. "Cordes checked into the College Inn at ten fifteen last night. The switchboard operator said he tried to place a few local calls around ten twenty-five, but the numbers he was trying seemed to be busy. In any case, he placed four or five calls in very quick succession."

"At some point in here he seems to have unpacked. Then, he went down to the bar. That was," and the chief consulted his notes again, "about ten forty-five."

"He had a beer, but when he found they were no longer serving dinner he went to the lobby and asked the night manager where he could get something to eat. The manager suggested that he try one of the places along the strip in Springfield, which is, apparently, what he did. In any case, he left the inn about eleven p.m.

"He got back at around twelve thirty, the night clerk thinks, and at exactly 12:55 he called the front desk, left a wake-up call for nine a.m., and, apparently, went to bed. When he didn't respond to the wake-up call, they had the maid check his room. She found him."

"What happened . . . I mean, how was he killed?" I wasn't sure I really wanted to know.

"There were two entry wounds, very close together, below his left ear. Small caliber bullets. Twenty-two or twenty-five. He was in bed. Probably never woke up."

"Jesus." That was all I could get out. "*Jesus.*"

The chief looked at me for a moment, then nodded and continued, "So the manager of the inn called me, and I called the sheriff and the coroner. I think Doc Fredericks will have the autopsy results later this afternoon. But it's pretty obvious what killed him.

"After the lab people left, I searched the room myself. It didn't look as if any of his valuables had been taken. His wallet was still in his coat pocket and his watch was still on the night table.

"But it did look like someone had been through his

briefcase. I was having trouble making any sense out of any of it until I found a manila envelope on the floor with your name on it."

"My name? What was in it?"

"Nothing."

III

As I was explaining how I knew Arturo, it occurred to me that he may have tried to contact me. The chief had said he tried to make some local calls around 10:30 last night. My phone had been busy then. In any case, I could hardly imagine that he would pass anywhere near here without contacting me. What I couldn't figure out was what he would have been doing here in the first place.

So I said, "He may have been trying to contact me with those calls."

"How's that?"

"Last night, between nine o'clock or so and eleven I was doing some work at home using the university computer. So my phone would have been busy if he had tried to call me then."

The chief looked at me for a minute, then asked, "Do you think that the purpose of his trip was to see you?"

"I don't know, chief. It's possible, I suppose, but I would have expected some advance notice from him if he was planning to be here. It really isn't quite like him to skulk around like a spy in some paperback novel." The minute I said it, I realized that was exactly what he had been doing. But why?

"Can you think of any other reason why he would

8

have been traveling through this part of the country?" the chief asked.

"There are any number of possible explanations. He could have been on his way from Boston or New York. There are a lot of reasons why an employee of the Mexican Finance Ministry might have been traveling around here." If you only knew, I thought. If you only knew. For a minute my mind drifted again. But I was able to continue with my thought, "We're not exactly on a direct path between all those places, but we aren't in St. Louis either."

"I know where we are, sir. But what I'm not quite sure of is what you mean when you say that there were a lot of reasons why he might be visiting Boston or New York. You did say 'a lot of reasons,' didn't you?"

This guy is obviously no dummy, I thought. "I'm afraid so, chief. As I just said, Arturo was an official of the Mexican Ministry of Finance. The Mexican government is deeply in debt to just about every major bank you can think of, in New York, Boston, and all of the international banks in Washington. And they are having a very difficult time making their payments. Very difficult. So Arturo may have been visiting bankers trying to renegotiate loans. He may have been visiting people in Washington trying to line up help there. Billions of dollars are at stake. Billions and billions of dollars. That's what I meant."

"I see." The chief nodded. He was one of those people who nod as if they already knew what you were telling them. "Well, I guess that's all the questions I have for now. You're not planning on doing any traveling anytime soon are you?"

"As a matter of fact, I am. The president has asked me to attend the economic summit meeting in Mexico City. I'll be leaving tomorrow." The chief didn't respond. "But Mrs. Lincoln will know how to get in touch with me if you need to and I'll be back. Probably in a week or so at the most."

"Well, okay," he said. "It's just normal to ask people connected to investigations like this to stay in town until things are wrapped up. But, the president . . ."

"Anyway," he said, as he rose to leave. "Be careful, sir. I have the feeling that something strange is going on here."

The chief was right.

IV

This was one of those very rare occasions when I didn't feel much like eating. But I was supposed to meet Bob Smith for lunch at the faculty club. I walked across the quad through a couple of Frisbee games and around the students sunning themselves on the ever cut grass; some reading, some sleeping off last night's rush parties.

Bob was the son of a graduate student I had worked with many years ago. After his M.B.A. and a couple of years of frustration in his father's investment brokerage house he had come back for a Ph.D. in economics. "Beats working," he had said, with what I thought was a certain amount of insight. We had become friends and I enjoyed talking with him. He had a refreshing tendency to ask intelligent, naive questions and the courtesy to listen to my replies. Not a common characteristic among my colleagues, most of whom had lost interest in economics the year after they got tenure.

The faculty club was filled with the same familiar faces. Some nodded. I smiled and kept moving until I got to the corner table we always reserved. It afforded an appropriately remote view of the quad on one side and the river on the other. The rowing team was working out, moving up the river like a centipede, out-of-step this early in the year.

Bob was beginning to look like a professor. He wore a Harris tweed sportcoat with leather patches on the sleeves, rep-striped tie and, a beard. All that was missing was the pipe.

"Hi, Professor Marshall. Good to see you. How've you been?"

"Not so bad, Bob. Not so bad, at least until today. Have you ordered?"

"Yes sir, I ordered the usual."

"Thanks, Bob, I appreciate that," I said, as I lit my pipe. The thought of a double martini was appealing.

"So, what's up?"

"Well, I've had better days. I just heard that a former student of mine has been murdered."

"Murdered? Where?"

"Right here in town, at the College Inn, last night. His name was Arturo Cordes. He was a Mexican student I met when I taught there."

"You mean a Mexican citizen was murdered right here in town. I hadn't heard. What was he doing here?"

"I don't know for sure, Bob. But it looks like he may have been here to see me. At least that's what the police think. There was an envelope in his room with my name on it, and it appears that he was trying to call me last night. There's something strange about it, but I can't put my finger on what it is."

"I'd say you're right. It does sound strange. Do they have any idea who did it?"

"None at all, apparently. Except that it seemed to be a professional killer."

"You mean a hit man? Here in Denville? That *is* something. Geez."

"Yes it is. It certainly is. And on top of that it looks like the Mexicans are going to default," I said matter-of-factly. I probably shouldn't have told him, but I knew I could trust him to keep it quiet, and, besides, I felt like talking to someone. "I talked to the president this morning, and, if you read between the lines, it was in the *Times* this morning, although it's not official yet." He looked surprised. Who wouldn't.

"Jesus, you mean a unilateral *default?* A repudiation? I can't believe it. That would mean the collapse of everything, wouldn't it?"

"That's my best guess. It'll be a real domino game. That's what the president thinks, too. And, as you can imagine, he has ways of knowing." To say the least, I started to say.

"So why was he calling you? Is he after you to take the Treasury job again?"

"No, no, nothing like that. He just wants me to go to the economic summit conference and see if I can help out. I'm not really sure yet what, exactly, they want me to do. But I agreed to go."

"Default," he whispered under his breath. "That *will* be something. The economic summit conference in Mexico City at the same time the Mexicans are getting ready to default. That'll be one for the history books for sure."

"It will, indeed, Bob. It will, indeed." Our lunch had arrived. Two martinis and two Bison Burgers. I wish I could break that habit. The Bison Burger, I mean, not good for the diet I was always on. But it looked and smelled good. My appetite was coming back.

We took a sip of the martinis, then Bob asked: "So what'll happen if the Mexicans default?"

"Well, I suspect that if—or when—they default, it will, at the least, have a sort of domino effect. Surely Argentina and Brazil will follow. And that will mean that, if something is not done, almost all of the major U.S. and European banks will fail. And that, in turn, would essentially put a stop to international trade, which would put us into a worldwide depression that would make the thirties look like a picnic. Other than that, it's no big deal." With that, I finished my martini and studied the olives, trying to decide whether to eat them or not. Fifty calories each is a high price to pay. But, then, I'd be traveling tomorrow and could work it off then. There's always tomorrow when it comes to my diets.

"How in the world did we ever get into such a mess?" Bob asked, as he finished his martini. "I've always wondered why the banks let themselves be exposed that way."

"Well, I've wondered myself, but you have to remember that it's often just the simple unpredictable course of events, more than anything, that screws up even the best laid plans. Mix that with the fact that the banks are just trying to make money like everyone else and you've got all the ingredients of a good old-fashioned financial crisis. It all has to do with oil, I tend to think."

"You mean the petro-dollar recycling thing?"

"Yes, that's most of it, I'm afraid. That isn't the whole story, but most of it. You may recall, that I have often said I thought the system was heading for a crisis. We've managed to stall it off by rescheduling and refunding most of the Third World debt. But that's only been a stopgap. Just a finger in the dike. Now the problem has compounded, and I literally mean compounded, into a situation where a collapse seems almost inevitable to me. Mexico, especially, has been sliding backwards for several years now, and I don't see any way out of it for them."

"It all started in the early seventies, when the OPEC countries raised the price of oil. We paid them billions, actually hundreds of billions, of dollars and they sent us the oil we had no choice but to buy at the time. The Middle East provided fifty percent of our oil imports. Then they turned around and put the money back into the U.S. and European banks, which, in turn, loaned it to the Third World countries, some of whom, like Mexico, were depending on oil revenues to repay the loans. But, when OPEC began to fall apart and the price of oil began to drop, the bottom fell out of the whole thing. So, it's a classic Catch-22."

"So," Bob said, "Mexico was depending on the revenues from the sale of their oil to repay their loans. And the bankers assumed that their oil revenues would keep rolling in so that they would get their money back and turn a nice profit on the deal at the same time?"

Bob, it seemed to me, was getting a bit wiser in his old age.

"That's essentially it, Bob. But there is another key point, I think, which exacerbated the whole thing, especially in the Mexican case. As you know, the only way a

14

country can pay back foreign loans—which keep getting larger and larger as they keep compounding—is to do something to increase their export surplus. That is, they either have to increase their exports or decrease their imports. Or do some combination of the two. Increasing exports is virtually impossible in the Mexican case. Their major export is oil and, as you know, oil prices are way down.

So Mexico, at the urging, or insistence, I should say, of the IMF has cut back drastically on its imports. But, unfortunately, they are simply compounding their problems. The Mexican economy is so closely tied to ours, and especially to our technology, that it simply can't operate without imports of our capital, machinery, and so on . . . especially replacement parts, almost all of which come from here and, to a lesser degree, Europe.

"Actually, it's not unlike the situation in Cuba in the early sixties when we cut off economic relations with them after Kennedy decided Castro was a communist. Remember? Very soon their economy just ground to a halt as the spare parts for cars, trucks, buses, tractors, and the like—all of which were imported from the United States—were no longer available. So, as Mexico began to cut back on imports in a desperate attempt to meet its foreign debt obligations, the economy began to slow down, which in turn made it virtually impossible for them to keep up with the debts they were trying to pay by cutting back on imports in the first place. Therefore, they are now up the proverbial creek without a paddle, and, ironically, we are right there with them."

"So, what do you think can be done?"

"I don't know, Bob. I just don't know."

"But I'll bet you've got some ideas, don't you?"

"Well, I've thought about it a little," I said, as I signed the check. "But right now I've got some people to talk to and then I've got to get ready to go to Mexico tomorrow. I don't suppose I have to tell you to keep this to yourself, do I?"

"No sir, of course not. . . . But, sir, this may sound a little stupid, but given what you have just said, do you think I should sell my stocks?"

"Well, it might not hurt to have a little gold on hand, if you know what I mean," I replied, smiling . . . as I left. "If this thing breaks, gold is the only thing that will be worth anything at all."

V

I negotiated the quadrangle again.

Back in my office I called my broker. "Bill, this is Cameron. I want you to sell all of my stocks and bonds and buy gold."

"You *are* kidding, I presume. You really mean sell *everything?*" he asked, obviously surprised.

"I am *not* kidding, Bill. Do it, and do it today."

"All right, sir, I'll do it. But you must be out of your mind. Gold has been down for a long time now."

"I hope I am out of my mind, Bill. I really do hope so. I'm sorry, but I've got to go." As I hung up the thought crossed my mind that that's what some people would call insider trading. I decided to consider it a gamble, but made a mental note to myself to give it some more thought later.

Then I decided to make one more call. What could I lose, I thought as I dialed Jim Halerpin's number.

"Good afternoon. Central Intelligence Agency."

"Mr. Halerpin please. Economics section."

"Halerpin here." It was good to hear his voice. We had met when I was a Fulbright Professor in Mexico. Fulbrights are attached to the embassy so they get invited to all the parties. Jim was a legal attaché at the time which, everyone knew, meant he was CIA. Since he was an economist we had become good friends. Now he was something at McLean. I wasn't sure what, but I knew he had a way of finding out what was going on. Whether he would tell me or not was another question.

"Hi Jim. This is Cameron Marshall. How's it going?"

"Hi, Cam. How are ya?" he said. "Long time, no see."

"Well, I've had better days. How's the spy business?" I always kidded him about being a spy. And he always said all he did was read the newspapers, which for all I knew was probably true.

"Booming as usual," he replied. "What can a faithful government servant do for a taxpayer today?"

"Well, I want to ask you a little favor, Jim. There's something strange going on in my life, and I thought you might be able to shed some light on it." Then I recounted the story of Arturo Octavio Cordes and explained that I had to go to Mexico tomorrow for the conference. I left out the part about the president asking me to go.

"Well, Cam, that is interesting. You say Cordes worked in the ministry?"

"Yes, he worked for Muñoz. Or at least he was the last time I heard from him."

"Let me check around a little and get back to you. Where are you going to be?"

"At the Geneve."

"Ah, yes, I do remember. One of the best bars in Mexico City. I'll be in touch. And . . . Cam: be careful."

"You mean don't drink the water?"

"No, I mean be careful, Cam. Something doesn't sound right."

VI

Living in a college town in New England has its advantages, but getting to the airport isn't one of them. The university limousine helped. It had, as usual, arrived on time—six a.m. It is a two-hour ride to the airport and I hadn't slept much. But I thought I should see if the *Times* had anything to say. It didn't and reading in a car always makes me drowsy. As I dozed off, hoping the driver could stay awake, Mexico was on my mind, as it had been all night.

My first stint in Mexico had been in the late sixties. A few articles on Mexican development problems had helped get me a Fulbright Professorship at one of the private universities in Mexico City, which, it turned out, was the turning point in my career.

All the theories about hard work, diligence, and perseverance leading to success are wrong. It's mostly luck. Or at least some combination of luck, preparedness, and opportunity. Someone had declined the grant at the last minute, and I was the only other applicant. So, at age thirty, Ph.D. in hand and barely fluent in Spanish, I was a Fulbright Professor. My beard hadn't even turned gray yet.

In my dissertation I had argued that the problem of Mexican economic development revolved around a simple lack of capital, technology, and education. Input enough of these and the problem would be solved given that the other ingredients were already there: natural resources and a surplus of labor. That, it turned out, was naive idealism; but I was convinced then that it, and I, would save Mexico and the rest of Latin America. That was before I lived there.

Lucking into my predecessor's luxury house—four bedrooms, with a walled-in *jardín* complete with avocado and poinsettia trees and a Roman walk-in bath and a bidet. Ann, Becky, and I quickly settled into the new lifestyle—a far cry from our tiny house-on-campus at home.

The maid María came with the house. She earned one hundred pesos a week, which at the time was about eight dollars. The Mexican peso was worth eight cents U.S. in 1968. It was from María that I learned that it takes more than capital, modern technology, and education to develop a country.

For eight dollars a week, which was about a dollar more than the prevailing maid-wage—and a point of consternation for my Mexican colleagues, who argued that I was upsetting the prevailing wage structure—María arrived at eight each morning except Sunday, cleaned up the kitchen mess, cleaned the bathrooms, mopped the floors, changed the beds and washed the sheets, washed, dried, and ironed the clothes, did the shopping, fixed the mid-afternoon meal—the *comida*—rode herd on the seemingly endless hordes of delivery people who came everyday: the beer man, the bottled water man, the trash man, the paper man, the shoeshine man, the daily carwash kid, the gardener, and the mailman who dropped by about once a week—more often if he got a big tip on mailman's day.

By around five she showered in the maid's quarters

and hopped a bus home. Two transfers and she was in the small apartment she shared with a brother, a daughter, and her elderly mother. By Mexican standards she was well-off. She had a job and supported her family.

The brother was an unemployed chauffeur, who I could have hired full-time for, probably, fifteen dollars a week. But even for me that seemed a bit much. Although whenever I had to negotiate the Mexico City traffic in which stopping at a stop sign means you get rear-ended, I was tempted.

The traffic was my first introduction to Mexico. Mexican automobile insurance is a *must* if you are going to drive in Mexico. Your U.S. insurance policy doesn't cover you once you are past the border. So you buy a new policy from one of the ubiquitous agencies in the border towns. If you don't you run the risk of spending the rest of your life in a Mexican jail.

I was on the outskirts of Mexico City when I stopped at a stop sign before trying to negotiate my way into one of the *glorietas*—traffic circles—and was promptly rear-ended. The driver of the car behind was not hurt, nor was I but both cars were in pretty sad shape. Without emotion he got out and began surveying the damage, making notes while I was looking for my insurance papers and wondering how to call the police.

After a few minutes he said, "I'd say three thousand pesos." And he counted out the money and handed it to me. As I was trying to say something like "but don't we need to call the police" in my then-broken Spanish he simply got in his car and drove away. Having no other realistic alternative and not knowing what else to do anyway, I did the same.

Much later María's brother explained to me that

Mexican law dictates that *everyone* involved, including passengers, in a traffic accident is automatically arrested and locked up until the insurance people get things settled. Since this can sometimes take weeks, it's just simpler to settle the thing right on the spot. Otherwise you have to pay a bribe to the traffic police, then at the station, another to the higher ranking officers, and if you let things get out of hand, more to the judge. The higher up you go the more it costs you, so the rule of thumb is: pay off at the lowest possible point in the hierarchy.

My second introduction to the reality of Mexico came with the washing machine. María washed the clothes in the roof-top laundry room in a built-in stone sink equipped with a stone sandpaperlike wash board on which after regular scrubbings my Brooks Brothers oxford shirts were surviving about a month. So I decided I could do myself and María a favor by simply buying a washing machine.

It wasn't easy but I found one, had it delivered, and showed María how to work it. The next day I went up to the the roof to see how it was working. It wasn't. There was María scrubbing my shirts on the sandpaper washboard. I pointed to the machine; she shook her head and said, "It doesn't work."

"Sure, it works," I said, and I turned it on to show her again how to get it running.

But it doesn't get the clothes clean," she said matter-of-factly, as she continued scrubbing a shirt that was rapidly disappearing.

The washing machine, I imagine, is still sitting there, gathering dust. That was when I began to realize that it takes more than capital, technology, and education to change hundreds of years of tradition. From then on, much to María's consternation, I took the shirts to the cleaners, who for all I know probably washed them on a stone washboard out in back somewhere . . .

I woke with a start when the limo driver said, "What airline, sir?" We were creeping along in the traffic, near to Kennedy International.

"Mexicana," I answered, as I tried to settle back down to the *Times*.

The agent clearly knew what she was doing. A far cry from my first trip to Mexico in the sixties when the Mexicans had just begun to fly jets. That time around, the ticket agent turned out also to be the pilot. But things had changed since then, and I had developed a bit more confidence in the Mexican airlines. Even if they are never on time.

"May I see your proof of citizenship, señor, please?" she asked, in a pleasant Spanish accent.

I gave her my passport. "I'll need a visa," I said. I thought of speaking to her in Spanish, but decided against it. It would have seemed condescending, as if her English wasn't good.

"Yes, sir." And she began filling out the visa, copying the information from my passport. "Married?"

"Yes."

"Occupation?"

"University professor."

"And the purpose of your trip, sir?"

"Just a vacation." I learned a long time ago that it was just easier to be a tourist when you go to Mexico. Mexicans are always suspicious of businessmen, which partly explains their problem. Tourists they understand.

"Please sign here," she said, pointing. "And again on the reverse."

I signed. "Here is your boarding pass, señor. Enjoy

your stay in Mexico. Maybe next time you can bring your wife," she added with a twinkle in her eye.

"Maybe I will. Muchas gracias, señorita."

"De nada, señor."

Over the loudspeaker came: "Buenos dias, señores, Vuelo 562 a Mexico y Guadalajara ya esta listo aboardar. Hacen el favor tener sus boletas listas para el agente." And then: "Good morning, ladies and gentlemen, Flight 562 for Mexico City and Guadalajara is now ready for boarding. Please have your boarding passes ready for the attendant."

I found my assigned seat without difficulty since the plane was almost empty. Flights to Mexico, like flights to Hawaii, always seemed to me to contain a curious mixture of people. Tourists, dressed in their casual clothes, and young secretaries in their shorts and slacks who would find out soon enough that, in Mexico at least, only prostitutes wear shorts. Except at the resorts. And there were the ubiquitous businessmen in suits and ties looking uncomfortable. I hoped that they all had remembered their Pepto-Bismol. Two million dollars worth of research by the USDA had uncovered the remarkable fact that Pepto-Bismol is the best cure for travelers' diarrhea.

As luck would have it, I wound up with a seatmate, a young, serious-looking, business type. Looked like he was fresh from the Harvard Business School. I considered telling him that I was an atomic physicist if he asked what I did, as I knew he would, so we wouldn't have to talk about economics. One problem with being an economist is that almost everyone has strong opinions about economics, but almost no one understands it. Which makes it hard to talk about economics on airplanes, or anywhere, for that matter.

The plane was an antique Boeing 727. The Mexicans—legend has it—buy their planes used from Pacific Southwestern, which buys its planes used from United. Whether that's true or not this was an experienced plane. Most people don't understand that when you fly, even in the United States, you're usually renting some space on an airplane that has been flying—almost everyday, all day—for twenty years or more.

We taxied to the waiting line while the flight attendants—half of them young men—went through the safety routine. They didn't smile about it, like U.S. flight attendants usually do. It was easy to see why as I looked around the cabin. It had been repainted in bright Mexican colors: yellow, red, orange; but this crate was no spring chicken, even the carpet was worn. But it flew.

As we hurdled down the runway and into the air I couldn't help but notice my temporary neighbors, most of them trying to feign indifference by reading a magazine or a newspaper. They were all scared to death. Their lives now in the hands of a Mexican pilot who certainly hadn't been trained by the U.S. Air Force, as are almost all of the U.S. airline pilots. Where, I wondered, does a Mexican learn to fly?

For some reason we took a northern route, circled Long Island Sound then headed south. In the distance I could see Manhattan. It would be a while before I saw it again.

"So, what brings you to Mexico?" my seatmate asked, after we had reached cruising altitude and resigned ourselves to spending the next three hours in an aluminum tube seven miles above the earth.

"I'm going to a conference." He seemed a friendly sort of chap. "And you?"

"Business trip. I'm with North American Chemical, and we do a lot of business in Mexico; but for a year or so we haven't been able to get any money out. I'm going to meet with our people there to see if I can find out what's going on."

"What do you think *is* going on?" I asked, just to see what he would say.

"I haven't the faintest idea."

Then, a few moments of silence as he studied his newspaper. But finally, "So what do you do?"

"I'm an international economist," I said, knowing it was a mistake.

"So you must travel a lot?"

Everyone thinks that international economists travel a lot. It just seems logical, I guess. Actually most international economists never leave Manhattan. Most of their time is spent monitoring exchange rates on a computer terminal. The yen drops a point and with a few keystrokes somebody makes a million dollars. An hour later somebody loses a million. It's all in a day's work.

"Would you like some coffee, señores?" the flight attendant asked.

"Yes, black, please," I replied.

"I'll have tea, please," my seatmate said.

Turning toward him I said, "I'm Cameron Marshall."

"Mike Edwards," he said, as we shook hands. "Marshall. Cameron Marshall? That name sounds familiar."

"Well, there are a lot of Marshalls around."

"Geez . . . now I remember. The guy who wrote the textbook we used in my international economics course was named Cameron Marshall. Is that you?"

I never understood why writing a textbook seems to

make you a celebrity in some people's minds, but it does. There's no doubt about that. I had autographed probably a thousand copies of that book.

"Well, if the last name was Marshall and the first name was Cameron, then it was probably me. I have done a couple of textbooks."

"Well, I remember it clearly. It was a tough book, but I learned a lot from it. In fact, I still have my copy."

"I'm pleased to hear that. It's always a good idea to keep your textbooks. If you don't remember something at least you know where to look it up. Textbooks you've used in a class are an extension of your mind."

Our coffee and tea had arrived, along with the small hard Mexican roll they serve with everything. I had forgotten that Mexican coffee is *strong*. It even smelled like coffee. In the U.S. what we call coffee is—to a Mexican—just hot water.

"Maybe you can explain to me, sir. What's happening in Mexico? Our company is having a really difficult time there," he said. I wasn't surprised.

"What, exactly, is the problem?"

"As near as I can tell we are making a good return on our investment. But they keep devaluing the peso, so while we have a lot of pesos on hand they're becoming worth less and less and, what's worse, we can't get permission to convert them into dollars. Apparently the government won't allow it. So we're stuck with millions of pesos that we can't do anything with, and they're worth less every day. What I'm supposed to do is to see if we can get some of them converted into dollars. If we can't I'm afraid we are going to have to close the plant."

"Have you considered reinvesting them in Mexico?"

"Well, we've talked about that a lot. But the problem

is that we would have to expand the plant, or add a new line, or something like that. If we did that we would have to import a lot of new high-tech equipment, computers and that sort of thing. But since the government has put so many restrictions on imports, that's almost impossible these days. We're having enough trouble just getting the spare parts we need to keep the plant going as it is. In fact, we've had to close down three lines and lay off a lot of the workers already. The weird thing is, we could sell more if we could just produce it. I don't understand it. Why are they doing that? It seems stupid to me."

"It does seem a bit strange, I must admit. But it makes a certain amount of sense if you look a little more carefully at what's been happening to Mexico over the past few years. They've gotten themselves into a real bind, and I'm not sure that they're going to get out of it any time soon. The interesting thing is that it's not entirely their fault. Like most of the underdeveloped countries they are just victims of a system over which they don't have any control. The short version of the story is that they've over-extended themselves and borrowed more than they can ever even think about paying back."

"But I thought they were overflowing with oil," Mike said, seeming puzzled. "Can't they use their oil revenues to pay their debts?"

"Well, that's what they thought at one time, but it hasn't turned out to be that simple. You've heard of petro-dollar recycling?" I asked, knowing that he probably had, but that he probably didn't really understand it.

"A little, I think, but it's been a while and I'm fuzzy on the details. It has to do with the Arab oil thing, doesn't it?"

"Yes, that's it. Remember in the early seventies

when the oil cartel–OPEC—almost collapsed the world economy?"

"Yeah, sure, they thought they had a monopoly on oil and they raised the price sky high and we had to pay it. I remember waiting in line just to get ten gallons of gasoline. That's when gas stations stopped washing windshields."

"That's right. There were billions of dollars involved; actually, hundreds of billions. They sent us the oil and we paid for it in dollars. Then they redeposited the dollars in U.S. and European banks and the banks, in turn, loaned it out to the developing countries. That is what is called petro-dollar recycling. The banks simply recycled the oil money to the Third World. At the time, it made sense because the developing countries were the ones that needed the capital to finance their own development and the demand for loans in the industrialized world was way down because of the recession caused mostly by the higher oil prices." I knew I shouldn't get started on this. I had briefing papers to read.

"So, where does Mexico come into this?" he asked. "Why would they need to borrow capital when they were sitting on all that oil?"

"Well, that's what makes the Mexican case interesting. It wasn't until 1977 that they found out that they had so much oil. By then López Portillo was in power and he had some very ambitious plans for the country—and for himself, I might add. He thought, and most people at the time agreed, that he could borrow whatever he needed to finance his grandiose development plans and simply pay back the loans with oil revenues. And the bankers agreed. They thought that Mexico was a better credit risk than most of the developing countries and so they were handing out money all over the place. From nineteen seventy-seven to eighty-five the Mexican foreign debt almost quadrupled—from twenty-five billion to around one hundred billion dollars."

"But I still don't understand why they can't just repay their loans from their oil revenues."

"Well, you would think they could. And I can guarantee you that there are a lot of nervous bankers who wish they could. But there's just one little problem. It's clear to everyone now—in hindsight—that OPEC had set the price of oil way too high for long-run market conditions. What happened was that they simply miscalculated the continued demand for oil. They thought we would pay almost any price for it, but, as it turns out, they were wrong. People reacted to the high prices with conservation measures, producing smaller, gas-efficient cars, and so on. And, besides that, the higher market prices stimulated our own oil production. On top of that, the cartel began to fall apart as other countries, notably Nigeria and Great Britain, discovered that they had some oil, too. The net result of all this was that the bottom fell out of the oil market and Mexico, among others, was left holding the bag."

"You mean because Mexico was depending on the income from oil sales to pay its debts? Wow, that doesn't look so hot for us."

"I would think not, to be quite frank. The problem nowadays is that it takes almost all of their income from oil sales just to pay the *interest* on their debt. So they're having to export all of their resources and getting nothing back. In fact, if you net it out, more money is flowing from Mexico to the U.S. and Europe than is coming from us to them. The whole idea of foreign loans and investment is to provide capital for them to develop, not us. But that's not happening anymore.

"That was what precipitated the first big crisis in August of eighty-two. They didn't actually default then, but the Mexican finance minister came to Washington and announced that they couldn't continue to service their debt unless it was rescheduled. Things finally had gotten to the point that they simply couldn't pay—even the interest. But, as you know, when the chips were down we came up with some more fancy rescheduling which has prolonged the agony, for a while at least."

"That *is* interesting, I must say." Mike said. "But, what I don't understand is why the banks would let this happen. Why do they keep renewing the loans?"

"Well, think about it for a minute. What choices do they have? If even one bank—and there are more than five hundred U.S. banks involved in Mexico alone—refused to renew even one loan, that would certainly set off a chain reaction that very soon would lead to a default. And a default, of course, is what the banks fear the most. Many of them are committed in Latin America far beyond what is normally considered prudent; so a default would almost certainly precipitate a series of bank failures, just for starters. So, obviously, the banks have no choice but to continue renewing or rescheduling and hope that they can at least collect the interest. Banks, as you know if you are familiar with what's going on in banking today, are very fragile institutions. They are totally dependent on our confidence in them. They couldn't survive a Latin American default."

"Given what you have just said, I'd think that this would be the time that the International Monetary Fund should get involved. Aren't they responsible for things like that?"

Mike was a good listener, which is rare among the businessmen I have met.

"Well, of course the IMF is involved. In fact, they are the referees of the whole ball game. And that's part of the problem. The IMF is sort of like these credit counseling outfits you've probably heard about. You know, those companies that try to keep a family which has gotten itself into debt over its head from having to declare bankruptcy."

"Yeah, I've heard of that. A friend of mine did it. He made some bad real estate deals and finally had to get one of those companies to reschedule his debts. Then he paid them a percentage of his salary every month and they distributed it among his creditors. But, as I recall, it didn't work very well because he lost his credit rating anyway."

"As a matter of fact, he would probably have been better off just declaring bankruptcy, or at least taking a Chapter Eleven."

"Chapter Eleven?"

"Yes, that's where you're protected from having to pay your creditors to give you some time to get your financial act together. You get a certain period of time to recover from your financial problems, but you are under the supervision of a bankruptcy court judge. It's rather common in the business world these days."

"Ah . . . I don't quite understand how that relates to the IMF and Mexico," Mike said, looking a bit confused.

"Well, when your friend went to the credit counselors, surely one of the things they told him was that he would have to cut back on his expenditures and live on a restricted budget, which they probably worked out with him. And that's just what the IMF does for countries with balance of payments and debt problems. They will help out with temporary loans and that sort of thing, but only under certain conditions, which almost always involves a so-called 'austerity' program. The country involved has to cut back on government spending, increase taxes, and cut back on its money supply, and so on—all the things that one would do to slow down the inflation rate. Which really means drastically slowing down the economy. The idea is to make the country more competitive in the world market so it can earn the foreign exchange to pay its debts. This, obviously, is not a very pleasant prospect for most of the underdeveloped countries, to say the least."

"So that's what happened in Mexico?"

"Yes, in essence, that's it. Since they agreed to go along with the IMF plan when they rescheduled in eighty-two and again in eighty-seven they have been under a severe austerity program which is causing the government some very serious political problems. But, what's important for you to understand, since your company is having problems there, is that one of the things that the IMF almost always requires is that countries with balance of payments problems cut back on imports and do whatever they can to increase exports. And that's what Mexico has done. Since nineteen eighty-two their exports, mostly oil and gas, have remained almost steady, even with a massive devaluation of the peso—some 2500 percent—and they have also tried to deal with the problem by cutting back drastically on imports, which has given them the export surplus they needed to at least pay the interest on some of their loans."

"So the IMF program has worked out pretty well for them . . .?"

"That depends, I guess, on how you look at it. Some people, especially the bankers, seem to think that it's working out okay. At least they are getting back some of their money. But I'm inclined to think that it's just a very short run, and very shortsighted solution."

"Really? Why is that?" he asked. I was trying to eat the hard roll and keep the crumbs out of my beard at the same time. It was a losing battle.

"Well, I would think you of all people would understand. It's the very same fix your company is in, only on a larger scale. The Mexican economy is almost totally dependent on U.S. and European technology. So when they have to cut back on imports as they have been doing, what happens is that they no longer are able to import the high-tech plant and equipment, not to mention the replacement parts they need to keep their economy going, much less growing. The net result is that everything is grinding to a halt, as I think you'll see when we get there. And, even more important, as things begin to fall apart they begin to lose their ability to sustain their exports, which was the purpose of the whole exercise in the first place. So, the problems your company is having there are a rather clear example of the results of an IMF-imposed austerity program."

"Of course. Now I understand. We can't import the equipment we need so we've had to shut down part of our operation there and lay off some of the workers. As this happens all around the country the economy just stops functioning."

"I would say you've got most of it. The other problem is capital flight. A large percentage of the money that is loaned to Mexico ends up right back in the banks where it came from. They encourage the borrowers to use the money to open an account with them—like banks always do—so the net flow of funds to Mexico isn't anywhere near as large as it appears. The estimates are that if it weren't for capital flight Mexico would only owe around fifteen billion instead of the hundred billion it owes now."

"So, what would you recommend we do? Do you think that there is any chance Mexico will ever pull out of it?"

"I'm sorry, Mike. But I don't like to give that kind of advice. Unless, of course, I get paid for it," I said, smiling. "And, in any case, I would need to know more about the details of your operation there before I could say anything intelligent about it."

"Yeah, I guess I can understand that," Mike replied, but he seemed a bit disappointed.

With that I reached into my briefcase and pulled out a copy of the *Monthly Review* and said: "Here's an article on the Mexican situation which might help you understand the details if you want to read it. I've got some things I want to look over before the conference."

"Sure, thanks. I'd like very much to read it. You've certainly cleared up a lot of things I didn't understand before."

"Ah . . . nothing personal, but I think I'll move over to that vacant seat where I can spread out a bit. Would you like to share a cab into the city when we get there?"

"Sure, I'd like that very much."

I moved back a couple of rows and sat down across the aisle from someone who appeared to be a Mexican businessman. Moustache, sunglasses, plain brown suit, green tie, and a white shirt. I nodded, and he smiled, the way people do on airplanes. He was reading a newspaper and looked bored, but he didn't look like the type who would want to chat. That was something.

Once I was settled again, I pulled out the briefing folder they had sent from the White House. This should be interesting, I reflected, as I began to read. Stamped in red on the first page was:

PRIORITY CLEARANCE

TOP SECRET

EYES ONLY

UNITED STATES OF AMERICA

Executive Office of the President

To: Kral, Hammett, Marshall, Mitchell, Moelker.

Subject: Mexico situation report.

Imperative that action be taken immediately. Situation is urgent. Repeat: URGENT.

You are requested to be at American Embassy 0900 EST Thursday for further briefing, consultation, and assignment. Report to Mitchell on arrival in Mexico City for details.

Study attached background data and documentation carefully.

LACY

EXECUTIVE SUMMARY

CIA, MI-5 AND OTHER INFORMED SOURCES REPORT THAT DEFAULT ON MEXICAN FOREIGN DEBT IS IMMINENT. THE OFFICIAL ANNOUNCEMENT IS EXPECTED AT BEGINNING OF ECONOMIC SUMMIT CONFERENCE.

EXTREME POLITICAL PRESSURE FROM BOTH RIGHT AND LEFT WING POLITICAL PARTIES AND LABOR INTERESTS HAS BEEN APPLIED TO FORCE THE GOVERNMENT TO REPUDIATE ALL DEBT PAYMENTS, PRINCIPAL AND INTEREST, AND ALL AGREEMENTS WITH IMF AND WORLD BANK.

THE EARTHQUAKE OF SEPTEMBER 1985 FOLLOWED BY THE OPEC OIL PRICE REDUCTION APPEARS TO HAVE BEEN THE *COUP DE GRACE*. MEXICAN REVENUES FROM TOURISM ARE DOWN MORE THAN 60 PERCENT IN THE PAST SIX MONTHS AND OIL REVENUES ARE DOWN BY 50 PERCENT. RATE OF INFLATION IS NOW RUNNING AT NEARLY 100 PERCENT.

THE ECONOMIC SITUATION IN MEXICO HAS BEEN RAPIDLY DETERIORATING. INTEREST ON THE DEBT NOW EXCEEDS TOTAL OIL EXPORT REVENUES.

EFFORTS TO REDUCE IMPORTS HAVE BEEN MADE AND THE VOLUME OF IMPORTS HAS DECREASED BY ALMOST 50 PERCENT SINCE 1981. BUT REDUCTION IN IMPORTS HAS CAUSED INDUSTRIAL PRODUCTION TO DECLINE BY 30 PERCENT SINCE 1982 DUE TO UNAVAILABILITY OF REPLACEMENT PARTS, AND OTHER KEY INPUTS. ECONOMIC GROWTH RATE FOR THIS YEAR IS ESTIMATED AT NEGATIVE 5 PERCENT.

PESO DEVALUATION OF OVER 2500 PERCENT SINCE 1980 HAS FAILED TO STIMULATE EXPORTS. PESO MARKET MAY COLLAPSE ANY TIME.

EXCHANGE CONTROLS HAVE MADE THE PESO VIRTUALLY INCONVERTIBLE AND DOLLAR AND OTHER FOREIGN EXCHANGE HOLDINGS ARE NOW BELOW ONE BILLION U.S.

THE TOP 10 U.S. MONEY CENTER BANKS ARE NOW EXPOSED TO THE SIX MAJOR DEBTOR COUNTRIES IN THE AMOUNT (ON AVERAGE) OF MORE THAN 200 PERCENT OF SHAREHOLDERS EQUITY.

DEFAULT IS CERTAIN TO PRECIPITATE BANK FAILURES, PANIC AND COLLAPSE OF THE INTERNATIONAL FINANCIAL SYSTEM, AND COULD WELL CAUSE A WORLDWIDE DEPRESSION.

Well it looks as though they have finally figured it out, I thought, as some static came over the loudspeaker that sounded something like: "Ladies and Gentlemen, we are making our final approach to Mexico City airport. Please return your trays and seatbacks to their full upright position, and extinguish all smoking materials when the captain turns on the no smoking sign. Thank you."

VII

It's not so much that it's corruption; paying a little bribe for governmental services is just part of the way of life in Mexico. Nobody thinks much about it and it's built into the pay structure. There's even a standard fee for most things, two thousand pesos for a routine traffic violation—like speeding. You just be sure you always have some money with you when you drive anywhere.

For going through customs if you want to bring in something illegal—like a *Playboy* magazine—the standard fee is five dollars, U.S. The customs inspectors just stack up the money on a shelf in plain sight. No need to hide it. Since I wasn't bringing in anything even close to illegal this trip I had just put a five on top of the shirts in my suitcase, to speed things along in case they decided to search my luggage. This time they didn't and I cleared customs with a minimum of hassle and met up with Mike. "I think we have to go across the street to get a cab," I said.

"Okay," he said. "I'm with you." He was dragging two bags and a briefcase. Not an experienced traveler, that was obvious. As we stepped outside you could hear the city. It's a sort of deafening noise that never seems to go away. And there was an almost overwhelming smell of gasoline and exhaust fumes. I motioned to Mike, and pointed, "Over there."

As I stepped off the curb I noticed a cab pulling in and then realized it was heading right for me. Just then someone grabbed my jacket collar and jerked me backward. Whoever it was was strong; I almost fell. The cab kept on going and soon was out of sight. I looked in back of me as soon as I caught my breath. It was the Mexican from the plane.

"You have to be careful crossing the street in Mexico, señor," he said, in perfect English.

He wasn't smiling this time. All I could say was, "Thanks."

"Let me help you find a cab, señor. You can get a better price from the gypsies." And with that he raised his hand and a cab appeared from nowhere. "This should do it, señores," he said to both of us. "Good luck. And . . . señor . . . be careful."

Regaining my composure, I said to the cab driver, "Buenas dias, señor, vamos al Hotel Geneve. Se queda en la Zona Rosa. ¿Lo conoce?" I decided it was time to start speaking Spanish. Mike looked a bit surprised.

"Sure, I know it. No problem, sir," the driver replied. "I'll have you there in a jiffy."

I should have known better. "Okay, fine. So where did you learn to speak English so well?" I asked him.

"In California. I was a bracero for about ten years. Picking artichokes in Watsonville was my specialty. Pays better than tomatoes."

"That sounds like a lot of work," I said, still surprised, although I shouldn't have been. In Mexico, unless you're really out in the countryside you can always find someone who speaks English.

"Oh, it wasn't so bad. Especially when you consider the alternatives," he said, as we weaved in and out of the traffic, which was worse than New York. Except that people don't honk at each other all the time. That, I remembered, is because anyone wealthy enough to own a car in Mexico is also wealthy enough to carry a gun in the glove compartment. That tends to discourage people from honking at each other. The other difference is the pedestrians, who think that crossing the street is like a bullfight. The car, to them, is the bull and they are the matador. All that makes a cab ride in Mexico City an adventure in itself.

"So, how did you end up back here in Mexico?" I asked. I was curious to find out how someone who had been a bracero most of his life ended up driving a cab in Mexico City.

"Well, you know, I picked artichokes until I had saved up enough money to come back here and start my own business. It was a little copy shop. I bought a couple of Xerox machines—which were new here then—and we made photocopies for businesses and anybody else who wanted them. It went pretty well for a while."

"Sounds like a pretty good idea," Mike said. "What happened?"

"Well, my friend, it was a good idea, I guess. For a

39

while at least. But after that mess in eighty-two we couldn't keep the machines running. Couldn't get replacement parts and the damned things kept breaking down all the time. Parts had to be shipped in from the States but the government cabrónes wouldn't let us have any dollars to pay for them. Finally, in eighty-three I gave up and sold the machines and bought this cab. So here I am. Sometimes I think I should have stuck with the artichokes . . . ah, hey, if you look over there to the right," he said, pointing to a vacant field that looked like a war zone, "you'll see what is left of the Hospital Santa María."

It was just a pile of rubble. "The earthquake?" I asked.

"Yeah, it was the biggest hospital in Mexico. Mostly for the poor people. I doubt if they will ever rebuild it. You'll see more as we get closer to the city. In some places they're making parks where the buildings were. They're just gone. Along with a lot of people and a lot of jobs. Two of my cousins were killed in the *terremoto*. Just disappeared. We never found them. It was very sad."

"Yes, it certainly was. It was a real tragedy," I commented, not knowing what else to say. "How has it been going since then?"

"Bad, señor, very bad. Before the quake, you know, I used to take two or three car loads of *gringo* tourists out to see the pyramids almost every day. Now I'm lucky to even see a tourist. They just quit coming. I tell you, I don't know what we're gonna do. Everyone is out of work, prices keep getting higher and higher. The pesos just aren't worth anything anymore. A bottle of beer costs five hundred pesos. Used to be two."

As we pulled up to a stoplight five or six men ran over to the cab. Without saying anything, one of them started washing the windshield, and the others were trying to sell us an amazing assortment of things, newspapers, trinkets, sarapes. I took a copy of *Exselsior*, the *New York Times* of Mexico and gave the young man one of the Kennedy half-dollars I always brought along when I came to Mexico. The Mexicans still idolize Kennedy, whom they view as the last American president who understood them. The young man was obviously pleased, once he figured out what it was.

"¿ Un Kennedy?" he asked, smiling from ear to ear. "Mil gracias, señor. Mil gracias." A thousand thanks.

As we pulled away the driver gave his windshield washer a few pesos and said, "I get my windshield washed about ten times a day. That's all they can find to do, except to shine shoes. Most of them just sit around, hoping something will happen. But it never does. Just look at the sign on that wall over there."

¿QUE NOS PASA? was graffiti-sprayed on a brick building wall.

"What's it mean?" Mike asked.

"What's happening to us?" the driver replied.

We were on the Paseo de la Reforma now nearing the Zona Rosa. The Paseo, I had always thought, is one of the most beautiful streets in the world. The large palm trees and the statues at each major intersection make you feel like you are in another world. One of the statues, El Angel, had collapsed in the earthquake, but it was being rebuilt. The Mexicans take their symbols seriously.

As we turned into the Zona Rosa I said to Mike: "There's the American Embassy."

"It looks like a fortress," he said.

"It is a fortress. Among other things, all of the windows are bulletproof. Well, Mike we're almost to my hotel. The driver can take you on over to the Sheraton. It's just a few blocks away. If you get a chance, take some time to enjoy the Zona Rosa while you're here."

"Doesn't that mean pink zone? Is it a red light district?" he asked, smiling somewhat uncomfortably.

"Not in Spanish. Actually the Zona Rosa is one of the most cosmopolitan areas in the world. You'll have a hard time finding Mexican food here, but the restaurants are excellent. Anything you want . . . German food, Swiss, Italian, Greek, Chinese . . . anything; there's even a Denney's in case you get homesick." I don't think he was sure if I was kidding or not. "Best of luck with your little mission here. I hope everything works out for you.

"By the way, there are a couple of things you might want to remember while you are here: everybody will be trying to sell you something wherever you go, but if you just hold up your index finger and wave it back and forth they'll usually leave you alone. Also, when you get to your hotel they will probably never have heard of you, even if you have a reservation. So just give the clerk at the desk a five-dollar bill. That helps refresh their memory . . . and, for sure, whatever you do, *don't drink the water*. Try the beer. It's good. Especially the Bohemia."

"Thank you, sir. I'll try it. Well, I certainly enjoyed meeting you. I hope your conference goes well."

"Thanks," I said. And we shook hands as I got out of the cab.

As soon as my feet hit the ground a young boy was shining my shoes. I waved my finger back and forth and said: "Gracias, no. No, gracias." But he kept on as if he didn't hear me until the driver said, crisply:

"¡Largate! ¡Largate, muchacho!" and the boy walked

away, mumbling under his breath, clearly angry and disappointed.

Then I said to the driver, "Well, my friend, Buena suerte. Que te vaya bien." And I handed him a ten-dollar bill.

He smiled and said, "Muchas gracias señor. Soy su servidor. If you want a taxi while you are here just call this number and I or one of my cousins will pick you up right away." And he handed me a business card. FELIPE GARCIA: LUXURY TRANSPORTATION SERVICE

"Thanks, I'll remember that. See you."

The Geneve—or The Genova as the locals call it—was one of the few large hotels in the Zona Rosa which had retained its Mexican identity, even though it was now owned by Quality Inns of America. The huge, atmospheric bar in the back was a most pleasant place. I had enjoyed many an evening there with Jim Halerpin talking economics and politics even though we never agreed on anything. He was an ardent conservative sometimes to the point of being a little spooky about it, I had sometimes thought. The bar was like an atrium with palm trees and other tropical plants and a high stained-glass ceiling. It was a good place for a quiet conversation, especially with a couple of Bohemias. I stepped up to the desk and said: "I'm Cameron Marshall. I have a suite reserved."

The clerk began thumbing through some papers rather officiously and said, "I'm sorry, sir, we don't seem to have anything in that name."

I handed him a five-dollar bill. He grinned, put it in his pocket, and began looking through the papers again. Then he said: "I am very sorry, señor, but there is nothing here in your name."

"Well, do you have *anything?*" I asked, trying to maintain my composure.

"No, we are full until the first of next week. Not even a suite."

I handed him another five and said, "Well, maybe you could keep looking. Perhaps there has been a late cancellation."

"You want a suite?" he then asked, becoming businesslike all of a sudden.

"Yes, that's what I said."

"Oh, why didn't you say so? We have just one left. It is 60,000 pesos a day. Will that be cash or credit card?"

On the elevator up to the room I asked the bellhop, "So the hotel is full, huh?"

"Oh, no sir, there's almost nobody here at all. Hasn't been since the earthquake. It's been very slow since then."

VIII

It was almost four p.m. Time for a little detective work. José should be back from comida by now. If anybody would know what was going on it would be José de Jesús Muñoz. As I dialed the number I tried to get myself thinking in Spanish. Talking on the phone is the hardest. You can't see the other person, so you can't tell if you're making sense to them or not and you can't use your hands to express yourself.

"Buenas tardes. Banco de Mexico," the operator answered cordially.

"Buenas tardes. El Doctor Muñoz, por favor."

"De parte de quien?"

"Professor Marshall."

"Momento, señor."

"Well, *hello,* professor" José said. "It's been a long time. How are you doing? Are you here in Mexico?"

"Just got here. I'm at The Genova."

"Are you here for the conference?"

"Yes, the president asked me to come along and see if I could help out. There are, as you know, a few problems . . . ah . . . listen, . . . José, we need to talk. What do you know about Arturo Cordes?"

"So you saw him? Good. Now you understand," José replied in a serious tone.

"José . . . ah . . . he's dead. He was killed the night before last in Denville. I didn't see him, and I *don't* understand. What's going on, José?" I was beginning to realize that there was something very strange going on here.

"He's dead? Madre mía. Are you sure?"

"Yes, I'm sure."

"My God," José said. "We've got to talk. Can we meet tonight? I don't want to discuss this over the phone. What do you think if we have dinner somewhere?"

"Fine, José, that would be just fine. I wouldn't mind some Mexican food if there are any Mexican restaurants left around here."

"Well, maybe there is one. I'll have to think of the right place. Let me make some reservations and I'll pass by the hotel around eight."

"Okay, fine. And ah, José, do you mean eight real time, or Mexican time?"

"Tonight, professor, it will be States time. Eight o'clock, en punto."

It was time for a little siesta I decided. I needed something to clear my mind. This was going to be a long night.

45

Mexicans don't even begin to think about dinner—la cena—until ten or eleven. That was something I never got used to when I lived here. Afternoon naps were one thing I *was* used to. A fine Mexican custom, I have always thought. As I dozed off I was thinking of José Muñoz.

I had first met José when I was teaching in Mexico on a Fulbright. At the time my Spanish needed some work and I needed someone to tutor me and, especially, to help me with the economics terminology. The university put me in touch with José. We spent hours that summer working on my Spanish and talking about economics. First in my office, but later at my house and at the local cantinas. He was the one who introduced me to the bar in the Geneve. We became regulars.

He was the son of a grade-school teacher in Colima and needed the money I paid him, which he would always refuse at first, then finally accept. From him I learned a lot of what I know about Mexico. How to bargain with the taxi drivers, how to fend off the shoeshine boys, and how to eat unpeeled shrimp.

No matter how good your Spanish is, no North American can get anything done in Mexico unless you have a native along to run interference. So whenever I wanted some information I took José along. He would confidentially explain to the government officials that I was a muy importante persona and from there it was clear sailing.

Eventually he became like a son to Ann and me. On vacations he came along, getting us Mexican prices at the hotels and bargaining at the local markets. That alone more than paid his salary.

When I was asked by the embassy to help choose a group of Mexican economics students for a State-Department-sponsored tour of the States, I made sure he was one of those chosen.

Later, when he graduated I helped him get a scholarship to graduate school at the university and we continued our relationship, this time with me as the tutor of English and teaching him how to get along in the United States.

His masters completed with honors, he went on to Vanderbilt for the Ph.D. and eventually back to Mexico to work in the Finance Ministry. Since then whenever I wanted to know anything about Mexico I called José Muñoz. He always knew.

He felt, I think, that he owed me a lot; actually, it was the other way around.

A few hours later the phone rang. "Professor? Aqui estoy. A las ocho, en punto." It was 8:30.

"Okay, I'll be right down."

"How about Las Brisas?" he asked, after we had exchanged greetings. "It's no more than a moment from here."

"Yeah, sure, I remember it. That sounds fine."

Las Brisas had changed since I had been there. It used to have a genuine Mexican feeling. Open kitchen in the back where you could see the women patting the masa harina into tortillas. Now it was almost sterile—antiseptic—chrome, plastic, well lit. Like a big, cheap American diner. But José had reserved a comfortable private booth in the back and we settled in and ordered a drink. I had a martini with imported English gin—Mexicans just can't make gin, it tastes like kerosene—José a brandy Presidente. The waiter put tostadas and salsa on the table and disappeared. It had been a long time since I had tasted real Mexican salsa, but I wasn't in the mood for it now.

"I'm sorry, José. About Arturo. I thought you knew. Was he still working for you?" I didn't know what else to say. I knew they had been good friends.

"Yes, he was. I sent him to see you. That's why he was in Denville."

"To see *me?*" My God, now I was beginning to understand. "Why?" I asked, almost afraid to hear his answer.

Instead of answering, he asked, "You didn't see him at all?"

"No. He apparently had been trying to contact me before he was killed, but I didn't see him."

"Can you tell me, in detail, what happened?"

I recounted the story, ending by saying, "Obviously, my hunch was right. There is something mysterious about all this. What is going on, José?"

"And you're sure there was nothing in the envelope?" he asked, still, it seemed, not ready to talk.

"That's what the police said. Just an empty envelope with my name on it. Do you know what was in it?"

"Yes, I do. Do you know anything about Los Palos, professor? Los Palotes?"

"Ah . . . Los Palos? Seems like I recall that that is the name of an ultra-right-wing group here in Mexico. I don't remember much about them, except that as I recall they are a bunch of neo-Nazi fanatics. I never took them very seriously," I said, trying to remember where I had heard of Los Palos.

"Well, you're partly right. They are a bunch of neo-Nazis, but they are not a bunch of screwballs. They are up to something quite serious. Since you've lived here they have become an important factor in Mexican politics. What happened was that they got control of the University of Guadalajara, and somehow convinced the USAID to finance the building of a new campus. Then they started a medical school which specializes in training American students who couldn't get into medical school in the U.S. They charge tuition that is ten times higher than the regular Mexican universities, and run large classes, sometimes as many as a thousand in one class . . ."

"Oh yeah, sure, now I remember. They've had some publicity about that," I said, beginning to recall but wondering what this had to do with anything.

"And," José said, "that's just the beginning. They've channeled the money into legitimate businesses and used it to back political candidates. They are now the major behind-the-scenes backers of the PAN. And they've infiltrated everything, especially the government. People who criticize them tend to end up dead, or just disappear."

"You mean, like Arturo?"

"That's exactly what I mean. I found out—never mind how—that they are trying to push the country into default and then engineer a coup to put the PAN into power. What I sent Arturo to give you was documented proof of what they plan to do."

"But why me?"

"I told you, professor, that they are everywhere. I couldn't risk going through the regular channels. I was hoping that if you got the documentation you could get it to President Dawson. So I sent Arturo. They have to be stopped before the default."

"*Before the default?*" I asked, not believing what I was hearing. "You're going to default? For sure?"

"This is very confidential," he said in a lowered voice. "But I think Córdoba is going to announce it during his opening speech Friday. Yes we are going to default. There's no other route."

I wasn't surprised, but hearing him actually say it still numbed me. I felt like the whole world had gone mad.

"Our foreign exchange reserves are almost nothing, and the IMF has canceled all further credit because we are not in compliance with their stupid austerity program. We can do nothing. It was the quake, of course, that finally did it. But with the prices of petro falling the way they have recently, it was just a little time anyway. The people are not going to have any more austerity. If we don't do something now, there will be a revolution, or, even worse, a coup engineered by Los Palos. And you already know what that would mean."

"Yes, I know. But what do you think can be done? It sounds like you're saying you want a default but, at the same time, want to keep Los Palos from taking over."

"I don't know. I really don't know what can be done. But I tell you this: nothing could be worse than it is now. Sometimes it's just better to be bankrupt. At least then we can start over with a clear blackboard. That would be better than going backwards, which is what we have been doing for the last ten years."

"Well, I can certainly understand that, and I really can't say that I disagree with you. In your place I would probably do the same thing. But surely Argentina, Brazil, and the others are going to follow. And that's going to mean the collapse of the whole system. Don't you agree? And without credit and U.S. imports it's all over for Latin America."

"I am in agreement that the others will follow," he said. "In fact, we've been talking with them. They will announce immediately after we do. But President Córdoba thinks we'll be able to get credit. He thinks we'll get it, if it's necessary."

"From where?" I asked, getting a sinking feeling in the pit of my stomach. Now I knew why the president had been so concerned.

"From the Russians," he replied matter-of-factly. "If it's necessary. But I doubt that it will be."

"Does Córdoba know about the expected coup?"

"I doubt it. We've tried to tell him but he won't believe us. But now perhaps you can see his strategy. There has to be some way to make the U.S. see that this situation is no longer workable, tolerable, or acceptable. The IMF, especially, just played out its hand too far, and we are calling their bluff. Can you understand that we simply have no other alternative?"

"So where do you fit into all this?"

"I agree that a default is necessary. It's inevitable anyway. But I, and many others certainly aren't ready to turn the country over to Los Palos. That's why I sent Arturo to see you."

"So what do you want me to do?"

"We want you to buy out the debt."

"Are you serious, José?"

"Yes, I'm very serious. Do you want a neo-Nazi Fascist state right on your border . . . another Chile?"

"That will never happen. You know Dawson would never allow it."

"Now do you understand?" José asked.

"Yes, I can understand . . . look, José, can you do me a favor?"

"Of course. I'm at your service. What would you like me to do?"

"Get me in to see Gómez-Hil." I had to find out what was going on.

"When?"

"Tomorrow."

"That's going to be difficult, taking into account everything. Is it official or private?"

"Very much off the record."

"Well, let me see what I can do, and I'll call you tomorrow in the morning. Where will you be?"

"At the embassy. And . . . José, let's keep this very quiet, okay?"

"Okay, professor, but there's one more thing you should know."

"What is that?" I asked, wondering how there could be more.

"Gómez is a Palo. Here is a copy of the letter Arturo was supposed to give you. Everything is documented. You've got to get this to President Dawson."

I had been so surprised by what José had been saying that I had forgotten all about the envelope that had cost Arturo Octavio Cordes his life. I took it, put it in my inside coat pocket, and said, "I will, José. As soon as I can. You have my word on that."

"Read it tonight, professor, then you will understand. And . . . professor," he paused and looked around the room, "be careful."

"Sounds to me like you had better be careful yourself, José."

"Yes, I know," he said as he stood up.

As we left the restaurant I glanced to my right. In a front booth eating and reading a newspaper was the Mexican who had pulled me out of the way of the cab at the airport. My first inclination was to go over and say something to him. Then I decided it would be a mistake; but I knew it was no coincidence this time. He ignored me.

Back in the security of my suite again I settled into the not-very-comfortable overstuffed couch and opened the envelope José had given me. It was apparently a copy of what Arturo had been trying to deliver to me.

My dear Professor,

I know you will be surprised to receive this communication from me in this unusual manner, but after you read it you will understand that there was no other way. It is imperative that this information and the documentation enclosed gets to President Dawson directly and personally. It cannot go through the regular channels, either here or there. You must deliver it to him personally and quickly.

As you know, our country is ready to collapse. In the matter of only a very short time the government will be forced to unilaterally default on the foreign debt. Some of us who are active in the liberal wing of the PRI have been attempting to work out a compromise solution, but it has been to no avail. The default will come soon and I for one have come to believe that it may be the only solution, if it were but that simple. But, unfortunately, it's not. Hence, the reason for my communicating with you in this fashion.

Certain functionaries who are connected to the presidential offices and our *Servicio Secreto,* and who are connected to our cause, have discovered that a group of Nazi sympathizers who have connections with and financial support from extreme right-wing interests in the United States are attempting to take advantage of the economic problems to engineer a *coup d'etat* of the government. Their goal is to force the government into a default. When that happens they will try to take charge amid the chaos that will certainly result. They will use terrorist tactics to render ineffective the federal and local governments and will install a fascist-military regime.

They call themselves Los Palos, and they are headquartered in the state of Jalisco, in Guadalajara. Their base of operation is the university there, which they have controlled and used as a terrorist training center for many years now. The university was, as you may recall, funded by the U.S. government.

We do not know who their leaders are but we have reason to suspect that there are strong connections between them and the U.S. Central Intelligence Agency, hence, the reason that these materials must be delivered to President Dawson personally.

We do know, however, that they have managed to put members of their group into almost every Mexican governmental agency. A list of those operatives is attached along with copies of other documentation of their activities and plans. When you see these documents you will understand the gravity of the situation.

Please act quickly, professor. There is very little time.

Attentively,

José de Jesús Muñoz

I thumbed through the documents quickly. There were plans to disable the Rancho Verde nuclear power plant, to blow up the major refineries, to mine the harbors, and to close the airports by mining the runways. And more. Much more.

The list of people involved was more than three pages long. Some state governors, most of the officials at the university, and two cabinet members. One name jumped off the page: Manuel Gómez-Hil, minister of finance. My old friend from Cambridge, "believed to be in line to take over the presidency after the coup." And I had thought I should see him tomorrow, thought he could tell me what was happening. He could indeed, it looked like.

What to do next I didn't know. The president wouldn't be here until the day after tomorrow and I certainly couldn't risk sharing this with anyone else. Only one thing was obvious: I had to put this stuff somewhere it would be safe. Then my mind flashed back to Denville and Arturo. Los Palos already had it. But they didn't know I did.

One thing I had learned from my tour with Air Force intelligence was how to hide something. There were a thousand ways: put it in the hotel safe—too obvious; put it under my pillow, under the rug, in the mattress—all too corny. Usually the best place to hide something is just not to hide it at all.

I put the envelope in my briefcase in the file with the briefing papers the president had sent me and just laid it on the chair next to my bed.

IX

After one of those nights where you think you didn't sleep at all but know that you did because your thoughts drifted in and out of being rational, I bolted out of bed when my travel alarm went off at seven. I showered and dressed quickly. Then I froze. The briefcase was gone. I had outfinessed myself.

Sobered by the turn of events, I decided to act as if nothing had happened. When you don't know what else to do acting normal is the best strategy. I had breakfast in the Geneve dining room. For breakfast it was one of the best in town, very authentic Mexican, juevos rancheros, real coffee, and all the fresh fruit you can eat—papaya, mango, cantaloupe, watermelon—all for 1100 pesos: or about one U.S. dollar.

Then I called Mitchell. I should have called him yesterday, but I didn't because I figured he would have wanted me to come to dinner. That wouldn't have been a very productive use of my time. Besides, I'd always thought he was a bore.

"Hello, Cameron. How are you, my buen amigo." He was one of those people who liked to mix a little Spanish into the conversation just to let everyone know he spoke it. The Mexicans despised him.

"Good morning, Mr. Ambassador. Lacy told me to contact you."

"Yes, I know. I'm glad you're here. Where are you?"

"In the Genova." Strictly third rate in his mind, I was sure.

"Well, at least you're close. Come on over as soon as you can. We're meeting at ten with Lacy, Hammett, Moelker, and some of the others."

"I'll be there in a few minutes."

It was raining, as it usually did this time of year, but I decided to walk anyway. I always enjoyed the walk through the Zona Rosa. Fending off six or seven shoeshine boys—successfully this time: you just have to keep walking—I was at the embassy in four minutes. The American Embassy in Mexico City is located right on the Paseo de la Reforma and right next to the Hotel María Isabel. A couple of blocks down the street is Chapultepec Park and the Museum of Anthropology. A tall, heavy metal-bar fence surrounds an imposing gray building with narrow vertical windows. It looks more like a museum than an embassy but it radiates a feeling of solidity . . . and power. Not a very inviting place, I had always thought.

Every day there is a line of Mexicans—extending around the block—waiting to apply for a visa to get to the States. To get one they have to show evidence that they are wealthy or that they have relatives there who are U.S. citizens. Almost none of them can do that, but they keep coming, day after day.

You don't just walk in. The well-polished Marine guards won't let you past the gate unless you can demonstrate that you have business to attend to. But they seemed to know I was coming. One of them escorted me to the ambassador's office where William Lacy, the president's top aide and chief of staff and Hugh Hammett, the secretary of Treasury, were waiting.

"Good morning, Cameron," Lacy said. "Glad you could come. The president told me to tell you he appreciated your getting involved in this mess. Have you met the secretary?" Lacy tended to be all business. He was a former stockbroker, who looked like one, gray hair, pinstriped suit, and wing-tipped shoes. He didn't smile much.

"No, I haven't. Pleased to meet you, Mr. Secretary," I said as we shook hands.

"It's my pleasure, professor. I've always admired your work. Just call me Hugh." He was a friendly, rotund sort of fellow, with a soft Southern accent; South Carolina. He looked more like a Southern state politican than a secretary of the Treasury. The ambassador wasn't there. They'd probably sent him over to the conference to shake some hands.

"When is the president coming?" I asked Lacy.

"Tomorrow morning. And we've got a lot to do before that. Are you briefed on all this?"

"Yes, I think so," I replied, wondering if he knew any more than I did. "It looks serious. Very serious."

"Have you heard anything from the Mexicans . . . ah . . . I mean, have you talked to anybody since you've been here?"

Hammett was listening carefully, but he wasn't saying anything. It was clear that Lacy was in charge.

"Well, just José Muñoz, last night. We had dinner."

"And?"

"It looks like they are going to default," I wasn't ready to talk about Los Palos just yet.

"Do you know when?"

"Tomorrow morning. Muñoz thinks Córdoba will announce it when he opens the conference."

"Do you think it's gonna be some kinda conciliatory thing or a complete repudiation?" Hammett asked.

"A complete repudiation, from what I understand," I replied.

"Damn it!", Lacy said. "I knew it. I just knew it. I tried to tell the president, but I think he thought they were just bluffing. He thought we could get down here and talk them out of it."

"They are *not* bluffing. I can guarantee you that," I said, as forcefully as I could.

"Listen . . . Cameron, do you think you'd be up for a little job this afternoon, if I can get things arranged?" Lacy asked. The way he said it made it clear that I didn't have a lot of choice.

"Of course. Anything. What do you think I can do?"

"Talk with President Córdoba."

"Córdoba?" This was a complete surprise. "I've already asked Muñoz to try to get me into see Gómez this afternoon. We're old friends from Cambridge, but I've never met Córdoba."

"That's okay. This is just going to be a little private meeting, off the record. Very unofficial, you understand. I imagine Gómez will probably be there anyway, so that may help. It's got to be off the record so that it doesn't look like we are trying to push them around."

"That I can understand. Whatever you say. Just let me know."

"Well, let's wait until after the meeting. Then I'll get on it right away," Lacy said, with some sense of urgency.

"It's after ten," Hammett said, looking at his watch. "We probably oughta get to it."

We walked quickly across the hall to the ambassador's conference room. The room was ornate, officious, and plush all at the same time. It smelled of cigar smoke. No windows, too much light. To my surprise there were only three other people there: Robert Moelker, the chairman of the Federal Reserve, Steve Kral, the CIA director, and Mitchell, who was pouring coffee for everybody. Moelker and Kral were talking quietly in the corner.

"Good morning, gentlemen," Lacy said loudly. "Can we get started?" Everyone sat down and waited for Lacy, who seemed to be in charge, to finish shuffling some papers.

"Everyone has the briefing papers, I presume?" Lacy said. There were nods around the table. "And you all know Professor Marshall? The president has asked him to sit in on this, as a neutral observer, so to speak."

"Sure, good to see you, Cameron," Moelker said,

leaning across the table to shake hands. I had worked with him on a couple of different projects over the years, and we were acquainted, if not exactly close friends. He was something of a conservative so we didn't agree very often, but I respected him, as did the banking community. He was one of the most powerful men in the world, but today he looked tired and preoccupied.

From the other end of the table Kral nodded and said, "Good morning, professor." I nodded back. We had met once at a reception. He was a retired admiral and still had a military bearing. Stiff and abrupt. But he gave the impression of knowing what he was doing. I wondered where he fit into all this.

"As you all know, gentlemen," Lacy said, "we have a crisis on our hands and the president wants us to see if there is anything that can be done about it. Steve, can you bring us up to date?"

"Well," Kral said, "we don't have much new beyond what you have seen. It now appears certain that Córdoba has been forced into a repudiation, and that they plan to announce it tomorrow afternoon. I doubt that there is any way we can stop it."

"And politically . . . what do you think?" Lacy asked.

"I think that if we don't do something soon we are in for some real trouble," Kral said.

"Could you be more specific, Steve?" Moelker asked.

"Well, specifically, our sources have learned that the Russians are going to try and take advantage of the situation. We've identified at least five new KGB people in their embassy and there is some evidence that they may offer some kind of new credit arrangement. Essentially, as I see it, it's the Castro solution. Default and get credit somewhere else if you need it."

"And," Lacy asked, "how do you think Córdoba will come out of all this?"

"We think," Kral said, "that at first he will be a hero in the eyes of most Latin Americans, but that after a default as the economy begins to fall apart, he will lose support and that may well mean that the Panistas would win the next election. For us, I hardly need to point out, that would be a disaster."

"So, from Córdoba's perspective it's either the Russians or the PAN?" Moelker asked.

"That's our best guess."

"But," I asked, "what would the Russians have to gain from a Mexican default? It seems out of character for them to be playing these kinds of games."

"I don't know," Kral said, "but they seem to be behind all of our problems in Latin America."

"Some choice," Hammett said. "That's a fine kettle of fish. Seems to me the Mexicans have got a lot to lose from all this. How can they just take themselves out of the international financial system like that? It doesn't make any sense to me."

"Actually, Hugh, it can be quite logical," I said. "A default can make a lot of sense when you consider the alternatives. At least, that's what the studies around seem to show."

"Make sense? How?"

"Well, first of all, it may make sense in the same way that a bankruptcy sometimes does—at least you get a fresh start; but, more than that, the repercussions may not be as serious as most people think . . ."

"But wouldn't we have to attach all of their assets?" Hammett asked, seeming upset. "How could they deal with somethin' like that?"

"What assets?" I said, smiling.

"Well, we could get a lien judgment and attach their ships, planes, and anything else that we could get our hands on. Especially the oil."

"Maybe," I said. "But, for one thing, you have to remember that that would just be a drop in the bucket. Also, you have to remember that most of those things are privately owned and that private companies are not liable for governmental debts. The key here is that seventy-five percent of the Mexican debt is governmental. Given that, what could we—or anybody, for that matter—do about it? We certainly can't seize their air force or their army, what there is of it. Theoretically, what we *could* do is sequester any funds the Mexican government might have on deposit in New York, or wherever, but, if I had my guess, I would bet that those funds have already been moved out . . . right, George?"

Moelker nodded and said, "Yes, that's right. As a matter of fact, that was one of our first clues that something was fishy here. And besides, you have to remember that the Foreign Sovereign Immunities Act makes sequestering funds a very tedious process, if not almost impossible. Also, sequestering is tantamount to an act of war. It might have made sense in something like the Iranian hostage case, but it surely wouldn't work in the case of Mexico—a friendly country right on our border."

"Of course," I said, "we could put on a trade embargo, maybe force them out of the IMF and the World Bank, or even cut off diplomatic relations, but what good would that do us? Unless we want to declare war, there isn't much else we can do. We will be the losers from this, not them. And, one of the things we may lose is a lot of oil. You have to remember that they are our largest oil supplier these days."

"So what we are trying to do here is figure out how to keep on getting oil out of a turnip," Hammett said.

"Well, Hugh, you do have a way with words," I said. "But I'm afraid that's about how the situation shapes up."

"All that aside," Lacy said, standing up and putting his foot on his chair, "don't they still run the risk of a complete breakdown?"

"Well, not really, especially when you consider the shape they're already in," I replied. "Most of the studies I've seen show that the actual cost of defaulting would be very minor, especially in the Mexican case. Not more than a one percent decrease in economic growth after a short initial adjustment period. In fact, in pure cost-benefit terms they have a lot of incentive to go ahead with it. Actually, we're the ones who risk the breakdown. Even if a panic can be avoided—and I doubt very much that is possible—my studies show that the U.S. economy would slow down by at least three percent in less than a year after a Latin American default just from the export trade we would lose."

"The biggest problem for us," Moelker said, "as you all know, is that our biggest banks have loans out to those countries amounting to more than one hundred eighty percent of their capital. And there is no way that I know of, short of nationalization, that we could keep our banks from going under. Even if we did take them over it would require a massive restructuring of our banking system to pull through it. Frankly, I don't think that it's possible. And I'm damn sure it's not desirable."

"So, how are we going to stop it?" Lacy asked. "Professor? Any ideas?"

"Well, I know that we are all aware that there are a number of things which have been done already to try and keep things under control. One way to deal with it is to convince the banks that it is in their best interest to keep lending even more money to allow the Mexicans to at least pay the interest on the old loans. Mr. Moelker and Mr. Hammett have had some success at that, but it clearly hasn't been enough. What's more, in the long run more lending just makes the situation worse. The loans compound and their debts just keep mounting.

"Another way would have been to increase the participation of the IMF and the World Bank. The IMF could have created a Special Drawing Rights fund for the debtor countries from which they could have paid their debts, and/or the World Bank could have increased its capitalization and begun making more balance of payments adjustment loans, which, as you know, it hasn't been doing very much lately. Either of these things might have solved the problem, or at least kept things from coming to a head . . ."

"Ahem, ah . . . professor," Lacy interrupted, "I'm sure that you could lecture on this all day, but that's all water over the dam now. It's history. We've got to come up with something *today* that we can do before *tomorrow* to stop this thing. What we need is a new idea. Something that we can propose to Córdoba *right now*."

"Well then, let them default," I said, just to see what Moelker would say. My mind flashing back to my meeting with José.

"But we *can't* do that!" Moelker said. "Besides, even if Professor Marshall is right when he says that a default wouldn't hurt Mexico as much as most people think, we have to remember what it would do to our banking system and our economy.

"Just think about the effects on workers in Providence, Pascoag, or Woonsocket if foreign borrowers do not receive sufficient assistance to adjust in an orderly way. What if they are late in making interest payments to banks, or can't pay principal, and loans become nonperforming or are written off as a loss?

"If interest payments are more than ninety days late, the banks stop accruing them on their books; they suffer reduced profits and bear the costs of continued funding of the loan. Provisions may have to be made for loss, and as loans are actually written off, the capital of the bank is reduced.

"This in turn reduces the banks' capital asset ratio, which forces banks to curtail lending to individual borrowers and lowers the overall total they can lend. The reduction in the amounts banks can lend will impact on the economy. So will the banks' reduced ability to make investments, which in everyday language includes the purchase of municipal bonds to help finance the operations of the communities where individual Americans work and live. Reduced ability to lend could also raise interest rates.

"I want to make very clear, gentlemen, that we are not talking here just about the big money-center banks and the multinational corporations. Well over one thousand five hundred U.S. banks, or more than ten percent of the total number of U.S. banks, have loaned money to Latin America alone. They range in size from over one hundred billion dollars in assets to about one hundred million. Those banks are located in virtually every state, in virtually every Congressional district, and in virtually every community of any size in the country. Those loans, among other things, financed exports—exports that resulted in jobs, housing and investment being maintained or created throughout the United States.

"If the foreign borrowers are not able to service those loans, not only will U.S. banks not be able to continue lending abroad, they will have to curtail severely their lending in the United States. Let me illustrate this point as graphically as I can. A sound, well-run U.S. bank of ten billion in assets—not all that large today—might have capital of six hundred million. It is required by the regulators to maintain the ratio of at least six dollars in capital to every one hundred dollars in assets. What happens if ten percent, or sixty million dollars of its capital is eroded through foreign loan losses? It must contract its lending by one billion dollars. Now realistically, the regulators will not force it to contract immediately, but they will force it to restrict its growth until its capital can be rebuilt.

"The new result in either event is one billion in loans that can't be made in that community—twenty thousand home mortgages at fifty thousand dollars each that can't be financed, or ten thousand lines of credit to local businesses at one hundred thousand each that can't be extended.

"And of course, this reduction in lending will have negative effects of financing of exports, imports, domestic investment, and production in individual cities and states around the United States, be it in shipping, tourist facilities, farming, or manufacturing. The impact will not only be on the banks—it will negatively affect the individual as well as the economic system as a whole. Higher unemployment and a reduction in economic activity, with all they entail for city, state, and federal budgets, would be a further result. None of this is in the interest of the U.S. citizens. Not to mention that we'd be in a worldwide depression within a month."

"Then I suggest you get Marchant and Lipsett down here right away," I said.

Jacques Marchant, the director of the International Monetary Fund, had been involved in the Mexican situation since the crisis in 1982. He was one of the early advocates of the austerity program that was now about to bring things to another crisis. Without his agreement, and without the support of Laurence Lipsett, the president of the World Bank, no plan had any chance of success. My hunch was that Lipsett, being an American, would be supportive. But they'd both have to be involved.

"Marchant is already here," Lacy said, "and Lipsett is coming in this afternoon."

"Have they been briefed?" Kral asked.

"Not yet, but I'll take care of that," Lacy said, "Look, folks . . . we've got to get moving. The president is going to want some answers when he gets here in the morning. So here's what I would like to do. First of all . . . Mitchell? Can you meet Lipsett at the airport?"

"Sure, no problem." It was the first word Mitchell had uttered during the entire meeting. He seemed strangely distracted by all the action.

"Bring him up to date and see if you can get him in here for a meeting at seven. Then, Hugh, can you meet with Marchant this afternoon? We need to see what he knows and how he feels about all this."

"That'll be fine. Maybe we can get together for lunch," Hammett replied. He didn't seem like the type to forget lunch.

"Okay, good enough," said Lacy, as he began gathering his papers to leave.

"And while they're all out running around, what are we going to do?" Moelker asked. He didn't seem too happy with the way Lacy was giving orders. Even the president's right hand man doesn't tell the chairman of the Federal Reserve Board what to do.

"Well, George, why don't you just stick around here if you don't mind. I'm going to arrange for the professor to meet with President Córdoba if I can and I also need to find out what he is thinking. Once we know for sure where everybody is at on this then maybe we can move. Okay? Everybody agree?"

"Sounds good to me," Hammett said.

"And, Kral, see if your people have turned up anything new. Okay? And we'll meet back here at seven sharp." With that Lacy walked abruptly out of the room.

As I got up I said to Moelker, "Looks like we are going to have to buy it out."

"You may be right, professor. You just may be right. Let's hope Córdoba will talk. Good luck with it. This is crucial, you know."

"Oh yes. I know. Well, we shall see what happens."

X

To my surprise, President Córdoba had agreed to see me at two. Mitchell had offered me the use of an embassy car and driver. But Lacy and I had decided that I should try to be as inconspicuous as possible. I hadn't told him about Arturo and the other things that had been happening yet. Sometimes discretion is the better part of valor. Besides, José had insisted that I talk to President Dawson directly. I felt I owed him and Arturo that much. But that wasn't going to make Lacy like it any better when he found out I hadn't told him everything.

I walked out through the embassy gates on to the Paseo de la Reforma and looked around for a cab. Before I had a chance to flag one Felipe appeared out of nowhere and motioned for me to get in. I was glad to see him but surprised and also a little puzzled. By now I should have known better.

"Los Pinos, señor?" he said, smiling.

"Yes, Felipe. How in the hell did you know that?"

"Nothing is a secret in Mexico, señor. I have a lot of cousins," he said, smiling again as he glanced at me in the rear-view mirror.

"That, I'm beginning to believe," I said.

The presidential palace—Los Pinos—is only about two miles from the embassy. But in the traffic it took us forty-five minutes to get there. I told Felipe to wait, although it seemed hardly necessary. I had been past Los Pinos before but never inside. It is a truly beautiful place, although not as pretentious as one would expect. It is set off, like the White House, from the reality of a ghetto only a few blocks away. But surprisingly there were no fences or walls around it.

Los Pinos is two large houses separated by what must be one of the most beautiful gardens in the world, exquisitely manicured and filled with tropical plants from all over Mexico. To get in to see the president you first simply ring the doorbell. I did, and a serious looking army officer answered and asked that I state my business. He then went back inside and I waited for what seemed a long time. Mexicans like to keep Americans waiting, I had discovered long ago, so I wasn't surprised. It's their way of letting us know who is on whose turf.

I was then admitted to a rather austere receiving room and asked to sign in. Interestingly, I was not searched, nor were there any metal detectors. From there I was escorted through a series of corridors and anterooms all decorated with portraits of heroes of the Mexican revolution. On one side we passed a large collection of guns, all gifts from visiting heads of state, my escort informed me.

Then a breathtaking walk through the garden to the executive house, which serves as the presidential living quarters as well as the executive offices. The smells and sight of the roses and bougainvillea were stunning. Then more corridors and anterooms, but by then it had apparently become clear that I had an appointment with the president and I had picked up an entourage. Finally, the president's office.

From what I knew of him Córdoba had always seemed to me to be a reasonable enough person, though he was rumored to be temperamental. A former minister of the interior, he looked like any government bureaucrat one would meet in Mexico, not at all the flamboyant personality his predecessor had been. He wore a plain brown suit. I had always wondered how he came to be "tapped" for the presidency.

A lot of publicity and rhetoric about democracy aside, there are no national elections in Mexico. The Partido Revolucionario Institucional—the PRI it's called—has maintained an iron grip on the country since it first came to power in 1929. Presidents are selected—"tapped"—by their predecessors from what is one of the best organized old-boys networks in the world.

After he is "tapped," the candidate travels frantically around the country campaigning—so to speak. Then an election is held. El tapado always gets elected with ninety-nine percent of the vote. It is, a Mexican friend once explained to me, much more efficient than the U.S. system given that everyone knows six months ahead of time who will win. The Mexicans have a knack for that kind of efficiency.

Lately however the right-wing Panistas—the Partido Acción Nacional—had been making some gains, especially in local elections in the northern border states and some were saying that the PRI was slowly losing control of the country.

I was ceremoniously ushered in by one of the numerous assistants. Large picture windows behind the president's desk provided a spectacular view of the garden. On the opposite wall were two portraits—Morelos and Hildago, the founding fathers of Mexico. There were chairs for eight or ten people and a conference table. In that ornate setting Córdoba looked out of place.

Gómez-Hil, the Mexican finance minister, was there as I had expected, and he acted as if he was glad to see me. He was heavy-set, with a moustache, graying hair combed straight back, and tinted horn-rimmed glasses. He wore a pin-striped suit. He looked older than when I had last seen him. It had been a long time. It was hard to imagine that he could be a neo-Nazi, a member of Los Palos.

"Well, professor, good to see you again," he said, as we shook hands. As is the Mexican custom, it was a limp-fish handshake. "Let me present President Ricardo Córdoba."

"Pleased to meet you, Mr. President."

"Likewise, I am sure," Córdoba said in English, which surprised me. There is a subtle psychological advantage in a conversation between two people who are bilingual that goes to the speaker of his native tongue; I was surprised he didn't take it. "What can I do for you, professor?"

I wasn't quite prepared to get down to business so quickly, but he was obviously not in the mood for the customary small talk. "Well, sir, as you no doubt know, there are rumors that you are considering a unilateral default. I was asked to come and talk to you . . . ah . . . to see if the rumors were correct, and if so, to see if there is anything that could be done to convince you to change your mind. Off the record, of course."

"Yes, I know. And I know why you are here." Then he looked at Gómez-Hil as if to say, "Should we tell him, or does he already know, or what?"

Gómez-Hil nodded, stood up, leaned on the fireplace and said, "Well, professor, I've known you a long time and I know you to be a man of honor. So, I am assuming this to be confidential to you and the others who you met with this morning at the embassy."

I knew the Mexicans had their own people in the embassy. But until now I hadn't realized that the conference room had probably been bugged.

"Yes, of course," I said. "We don't want leaks to get out any more than you do."

"Then," Córdoba said, "You should know that we are going to default. I am going to announce it tomorrow."

"A complete repudiation?" José, as I had assumed, had been right.

"Yes, a complete repudiation. We are canceling all debt."

"And there is nothing that could be done to make you change your mind?" I asked, still hoping he might be bluffing.

"Nothing," he said firmly.

"Professor," Gómez-Hil said, "in our place, what would you do? Do you have some magic solution to our problems?"

"Well, to be quite frank, in your place I would probably do the same thing. At least you will get somebody's attention. Can I tell this to President Dawson?"

"You can tell President Dawson anything you wish," Córdoba replied.

"Don't you think it might be better to put it off for a while? At least until after the conference?" I asked, probing. "It's going to cause chaos if you announce it at the conference."

"Look, professor," Gómez-Hil said, "can't your people see that this thing has gone far enough? We can't just kill all of our people to save the skins of a few New York bankers. We can not go on like this any longer. Just think about this: some twenty years ago Latin America had almost no debt at all; now it amounts to almost four hundred *billion* dollars. And where did all that money go? A large part of it was spent on weapons—especially in Argentina and Chile—and another large part was simply embezzled, stolen, and deposited in banks in Switzerland and even back in the states . . . some was squandered on stupid projects nobody needed, and, for some of the countries it was spent on oil. Only a small part went for economic programs that did us any good at all."

"Well, I understand that, but don't you think you

have a moral responsibility to repay your debts?" As soon as I said that, I wished I hadn't. I could see the anger swell in his face.

"A moral responsibility!" Córdoba exploded, standing up. Now I was the only one left sitting down and it was beginning to make me feel very uncomfortable. "First of all, these debts are not even ours. They were accumulated by my predecessors, and they are *not* my responsibility. Second, remember that when you are talking about nations you are talking about the people: the workers, the farmers, the students, the middle class—doctors, engineers, lawyers, teachers, and the other professionals. What did the people get out of the billions that were spent on weapons, deposited back in the U.S. banks, misspent, or embezzled? What did the people—my people—get out of all that? They got nothing. Absolutely nothing. Nada! And who has to pay for all that debt? The people: the workers, the professionals, the farmers; everybody has to make do with reduced wages and reduced incomes and make huge sacrifices." He paused, but the anger had not left his face. He was nearly shouting and needed a breath. "Where is the morality in all that? What is the morality of your imposing measures—these austerity programs—on us, which make the people pay for something they didn't have anything to do with? The people are protesting because they are being forced to pay a debt that they didn't contract for and that brought them practically no benefits."

"So," I said, "you think the people of Latin America will be better off by just not paying their debts?" I didn't like to be lectured any more than he liked having his morality questioned. Yet, again I regretted what I said.

Here was a pending event of immense international importance being shaped in part by two men unable to control their own tempers. Instead of answering, he sat down and nodded again to Gómez-Hil.

"Look, professor," Gómez-Hil said, clearly and successfully trying to control his temper, "you of all people must know that it's not just a question of wanting or not wanting to pay the debt. Paying it off is just simply a practical impossibility, a political impossibility, and a moral impossibility. Any democratic system that tries to impose the sort of restriction that would be required will be ruined. The debt simply can not be repaid. "Who was it—Patrick Henry?—who said 'Give me liberty, or give me death'? The choice for us now is between the cancellation of the debt and political death."

"But," I said, addressing myself to Córdoba and knowing I was losing ground, "do you honestly think it is realistic to expect the banks to simply swallow the losses from the canceled debt contracts?" My logic, it was clear, lacked the depth of his emotion.

"It's not the banks," Córdoba said, "who will have to swallow the debt. It's the governments of the creditor countries. The United States is not going to let its banks go under. You know that, professor, as well as I do. It's a simple accounting operation. And there are many ways it can be done. When you get right down to it, it's not going to close a single factory; it's not going to stop a single ship along its route; it's not going to interfere with a single sales contract on the market. To the contrary, employment, trade, industrial and agricultural output and profits would be increased everywhere. It isn't going to hurt anybody. So what if you have to cut back on arms and military spending? Who needs it? You already have enough to kill all of us thirty times over."

"And what if we don't agree?" I asked, knowing this conversation was about over.

"It doesn't matter to us if you agree or not. We are imposing a unilateral solution to the problem. And, as you will see, all of the other debtor nations will follow. There are no actions open to you. Economic blockades, invasion of the Third World countries, repartitioning of the world's territories and resources, as in past centuries, are simply impossible today. Any rational person can understand this. They can't invade ten countries, or blockade one hundred countries. Tell that to your colleagues when you meet again this evening, professor." With that last bit of defiance he stood again. It was clear it was time for me to leave.

"So, Mr. President, you are going to default tomorrow?"

"I will announce it tomorrow morning. We will default, and all the Third World countries will follow."

"If I could arrange it, would you meet with President Dawson tomorrow morning? I think there is the possibility that this can all be worked out." It was a long shot.

He appeared to think for a moment. Then, abruptly, said: "No, I will not. Good day, professor."

Gómez-Hil just looked at me and didn't say anything, but I thought I could see a smile in his eyes. More likely it was a glare.

XI

Back in the now familiar conference room I could feel a sense of urgency, if not panic, in the air. A Mexican waiter was serving coffee but there was none of the usual banter. Jacques Marchant, the IMF director, was there as was Laurence Lipsett, the World Bank president, along with the others from the morning meeting; except for Mitchell who, I imagined, was making arrangements for the president's arrival. I lit my pipe and settled back in the too-comfortable chair. This was going to be interesting, especially with both Marchant and Moelker here. I was especially interested to see how Marchant reacted. He had a certain French inscrutability, which I always found disconcerting. One key to this mess, I was convinced, was the IMF. They were going to have to give somewhere. Lacy, still apparently in charge, or at least taking charge as usual, opened the meeting.

"Well, gentlemen, I think you all know each other? So I'm going to skip the formalities."

I had never met Marchant or Lipsett but they nodded, looking as if they might be wondering what I was doing in a meeting like this.

Lacy continued. "I think you all know that Professor Marshall met off-the-record with President Córdoba and Gómez-Hil this afternoon, so I'm going to ask him to summarize what happened. Then we'll see what, if anything, can be done. Professor?"

I had already briefed Lacy, so I assumed he was playing out some sort of strategy. Probably he wanted to make sure Marchant understood the seriousness of the situation. "Well," I said, in my best, most serious lecturing voice, "there's not much to report. As we already suspected, they say they are going to default. A complete repudiation of all external debt. So far as I can tell Córdoba can't stand up to the political pressure any longer. He thinks he is going to have a revolution on his hands if he doesn't do something soon. By the way, I should mention that he knows we are meeting now and I had the clear impression that he knew what we had discussed this morning."

"You mean," Kral said, "that you think they have this room bugged?"

"That's the impression I got. How else could he have known what we talked about this morning?" I said, getting a kick out of the fact that our CIA director couldn't imagine that the Mexicans—or someone—had our own embassy bugged.

"Don't you have his offices bugged?" I asked, just to see what he would say.

"Well, sure, but that's different," he said, shaking his head and making some notes on a yellow pad.

"Could you check that out right away, Steve?" Lacy said. He was obviously perturbed. I had forgotten to tell him.

"I sure will," he said, looking embarrassed as he left the room.

"So, anyway, professor, you're sure?" Moelker asked. "And the announcement?"

"Tomorrow morning."

"Don't you think he might be open to negotiating?" Marchant asked, seeming surprised at what he was hearing.

"No . . . I don't think so. He seemed to be quite determined to go through with it. In fact he told me to tell all of you and the president that this was not just another bluff. I'm quite sure he will do it," I said as Kral came back into the room, still looking agitated.

"I'll bet," Moelker said, sarcastically. "So what does

Dawson think about all of this?" he continued, looking at Lacy.

"I talked to him just a few minutes ago," Lacy said, seeming a bit defensive and unsure of himself now.

"And what kind of a miracle does he expect us to come up with this time?" Moelker pressed. It was no secret that he and the president didn't get along.

"He said to think hard and pray a lot. Especially the latter. And he wanted me to remind all of you that God is on our side."

"Ah, ha! Jeez, that should help a lot," Moelker said, shaking his head. "I'd better notify the banks. They are going to be in real trouble when the news of this thing breaks."

"That," Lacy said, "is something they should have thought about a long time ago. The president said to just go ahead and let it happen. When it does, then he thinks we'll be in a better position to take some drastic action. 'The Indians,' he said, 'never attack at night.' So he thinks we had all better get a good nights' sleep. And I agree. I'll meet with him as soon as he gets here tomorrow morning, and get back to you. It's going to be an interesting day, gentlemen, a very interesting day."

As we were getting up to leave, Lacy motioned to me to wait. When the room had cleared, he said: "Cameron, the president would like for you to have breakfast with us in the morning, on Air Force One. They'll be in at eight-thirty. I'll have someone pick you up at the hotel at seven."

"Okay," I said, "Mexican time or American time?"

At first he looked at me as if I had lost my mind, but then he smiled for the first time all day, and said: "Eastern Standard Time."

XII

Whenever the president travels anywhere it's a major production. Three C-5s have to make two trips ahead, just to get the equipment in. It costs thirteen thousand dollars an hour just to fly one, and it's a six-hour flight. About three-quarters of a million dollars just to get him here.

Two presidential limousines are flown in—one for a spare—along with three bomb-sniffing dogs, two surveillance/medical helicopters, a cavalcade of Secret Service vans, masses of satellite-communications equipment, the president's private drinking water, and spare quantities of his type blood.

Including the press, the traveling entourage takes five hundred hotel rooms. Quite a production indeed.

I had been on it before but you can't help but be impressed every time you step aboard Air Force One. The entourage had already disembarked and there were only a few Secret Service agents left on board. Since I was with Lacy I didn't expect them to pay much attention to us. They didn't. They were sitting in the front section, which is reserved for dignitaries and members of the press pool, and seemed totally involved in a game of poker. One of them passed a hand to usher us past the bar and back to the mid-section where there is a combination office-dining area. Behind that is the president's private quarters.

The table was set for breakfast. Kral was already there, drinking coffee and looking over some papers. Lacy and I sat down, had some coffee too, and waited. We were early.

On the way out of the airport I told Lacy that José

had asked that I deliver a personal message directly to the president. He didn't like that at all, but finally agreed when I told him part of the story—the part about Arturo Octavio Cordes.

A Filipino attendant was refilling our cups and taking our breakfast order when the president appeared in the doorway from the rear section. He looked fresh and seemed in good spirits, but then he always did.

"Hello, Cam. Glad you could come," he said, as we shook hands. He was wearing a dark pin-striped suit, with a white shirt and a conservative tie. We all were. Slightly balding, but tanned and seeming fit, he looked like someone who enjoyed his job. I didn't envy him that, especially today.

"Good morning, Mr. President," we all said in unison.

It must take a while to get used to everyone calling you "Mr. President." It always reminded me of those jokes about what his wife called him in bed. He nodded at Lacy and Kral but didn't shake their hands. The Filipino appeared from somewhere with our breakfast: eggs benedict for us, with cantaloupe and orange juice; oatmeal, toast, and mango juice for the president. The attendant then disappeared as quickly as he had appeared.

With his mouth full of oatmeal, the president said, "Okay, gentlemen, let's get down to business. It looks like this is going to be a long day. Where do we stand?"

"Well, sir," Lacy said, "as I told you yesterday, it looks like Córdoba is going to do it. He will announce the default this morning during his opening speech at the conference. We expect all hell to break loose after that."

"Are you sure? Goddamn it! What the hell is the

matter with him anyway?" This was a side of him I hadn't seen before. That's not to say I was surprised.

I decided now was the time to get it out. So I interrupted Lacy, who was getting ready to say something. I said, "Well, sir, I think that what's the matter with him is that he's been the victim of a conspiracy. A neo-Nazi group called Los Palos has infiltrated the Mexican government all the way to the top and—I think—they've convinced him that a default is his only option. Then, after he does it and the country begins to fall apart they're going to try to engineer a coup d'etat." Lacy choked on his egg and Kral was staring at me, speechless.

"A coup?" the President half-said and half-asked. "How in the hell do you know all this, Cam?" he asked, looking at Kral. "And why didn't we know about it?"

Kral started to say, "Well, ah . . ." when I interrupted again. Then I recounted the story of Arturo Cordes, my meeting with José Muñoz, and the letter.

"That's amazing," President Dawson said. "Jesus, just amazing. What do we know about these Palos, Steve?" he asked, directing the question to Kral, who seemed to be recovering.

"Well, we know that there is such an organization and that they are connected with the private university in Guadalajara, and that they are well financed, mostly with our money. But I always thought that they were a bunch of tin soldiers. Or at least I did until Jack Anderson did an exposé on them last year. After that we put a couple of operatives in there. The first one was killed in an automobile accident—or what appeared to be an accident. The second, so far as I know, is still there, teaching at the university on a Fulbright. I guess we never took them very seriously. There are a lot of Nazi sympathizers in Mexico."

"What do you mean, Steve," Lacy asked, finding his voice again, "when you say they are financed with our money?"

"USAID put up the money for the new campus. The idea, as I recall, was to give some support to a university that would train students in our style of free-market capitalism. The Mexican universities, as you probably know, are pretty much dominated by Marxists."

"Jesus Christ," the President said, "you mean that we gave them the money to build a new university and now they are using it to finance a coup?"

"Well," said Kral, "if the professor is right, I guess that's pretty much what seems to be going on."

"Who do you think they have in the government?" Lacy asked me.

"Gómez-Hil," I replied.

"Gómez-Hil! The minister of finance? I thought he was a friend of yours." I don't think he believed me. Even I had hoped I was wrong.

"He was," I said. "We were at Cambridge together."

"But you just saw him yesterday," Lacy followed up. "Did he say anything then that made you suspect he was behind this?"

"Well, I was not exactly expecting him to be wearing a swastika on his lapel. But I watched him closely, and it was clear that he was the one who had convinced Córdoba that they didn't have any other choice but to default. Other than that, you'll just have to take my word for it that the documentation is convincing. But I *am* sure that José de Jesús Muñoz didn't just make this whole thing up."

"So," the president said, "what we've got here is a friendly country right on our own border about to repudiate all of its foreign debt, twenty-five billion dollars of which is owed to our biggest banks, and then a bunch of fanatic tin-soldier Nazis are going to try to take over the Mexican government. Other than that, things are fine." He wasn't smiling.

"What," Lacy asked the president, "do you want to do, sir?"

"Well, for one thing, Steve . . . I want you to get on this Palos thing with everything you've got. We've got to stop that crap. And I don't care what it takes. Just do it." His lips were tight and his voice steady, but like ice. "Then let's get to this damned conference. Where's Moelker?"

"At the embassy, I think, sir," Lacy replied.

"Tell him I want to see him as soon as we get there. Who's meeting us here?"

"Carrillo," Lacy said.

"Okay, let's go. And, Cam . . . thanks. But this time I hope you're wrong."

"Me too," I said. What else could I say?

Waiting on the tarmac at the bottom of the ramp was Jorge Castenada Carrillo, the Mexican foreign minister, and a line of other dignitaries. The president went out first. We waited.

From the door I could hear the president saying, "Well, hello, Mr. Foreign Minister. How are you? It's so nice to be here in your beautiful country again." He was smiling and beginning to pump everyone's hand. The motorcade was waiting and I got into the third limousine with Lacy. Kral was nowhere in sight.

XIII

The Paseo de la Reforma had been cordoned off and it was lined with Mexican soldiers. They were standing erect and at attention, spaced about six feet apart I guessed. They looked serious. Each carried a rifle and appeared ready to use it. But none of them looked to be more than sixteen years old, if that.

Behind them was a large crowd of curious onlookers, who seemed interested but not exactly exuberant. Some of them waved small red, green, and white Mexican flags. It was foggy and raining, but they didn't seem to notice. Only a few had raincoats.

I looked at the conference schedule Lacy had given me. Jacques Marchant, the IMF director, was presiding over a plenary session in the Aztec Auditorium at ten.

Córdoba, as the host, was then scheduled to make some welcoming remarks. This was, originally at least, just supposed to be a formality before the visiting heads of state met in a more private setting at eleven. Today, I suspected, it would be more than just a formality.

The Secret Service people got out first, and looked around, then the president. I followed Lacy in, through the spacious and ornate lobby, up the stairs to the auditorium. We walked past the press section in the back and on to the section reserved for the American delegation, and settled into chairs behind the president and Moelker who were whispering to each other. It wasn't hard to imagine what they were talking about. Moelker looked pale and drawn, as if he were about to faint.

Marchant stood up to the podium and the room became quiet. He said, "Ladies and Gentlemen, I would like to present our host, President Ricardo Córdoba."

As he came to the podium, Córdoba looked around as if to see if everybody was there. There was no teleprompter. He took some notes out of his inside jacket pocket and carefully arranged them on the podium. He looked shaken I thought, but perhaps it was just my imagination. He wore a dark brown, plain-looking suit, no pin stripes. As he began speaking, in Spanish, everyone put on their headphones for the translation.

"Ladies and Gentlemen, distinguished guests, and members of the press, I hereby welcome you to the beautiful, peace-loving, and democratic state of Mexico.

"As you know, these are difficult times . . ."

My mind began to drift away as he began to describe the great strides that Mexico had made during his administration. I should call Ann, I thought. She would worry when she heard the news. Maybe I could do that before the next meeting. Probably not.

Córdoba got my attention back when he said,". . . and the system is not working. It is extracting all of our wealth, the wealth created by the hard work of the Mexican people. We cannot continue paying this tribute.

"Therefore, I am announcing today, this same day, that by presidential decree we the country of Mexico will no longer use our resources to maintain an unjust and unfair system which has made it impossible for us to continue.

"We will no longer pay another cent to foreign interests and we will not be put in default. We hereby repudiate and declare invalid all foreign debt contracted by this government. This is effective now."

The first out were the press people in the back. They

hit the door at full speed. In a matter of minutes the whole world would know.

Córdoba left the podium and was saying something to Marchant who, in turn, was trying to say something into the microphone, but no one was listening. Everyone was standing and mulling about, trying to decide what to do next.

Lacy said, "We've got to get back to the embassy." The Secret Service people had moved in and were keeping everyone back from President Dawson, who was shouting something at Moelker. Lacy motioned to a Secret Service man and they began to escort the president out.

I managed to work my way through the crowd to the hallway and down the stairs to the lobby. Some reporters were crowded around the telephones, trying to read text to their editors. One from the *New York Times* who knew me yelled, "What do you think about this, Professor Marshall? Do you think it's serious?"

It was Mary Williamson, the *Times* Mexico correspondent. I had always thought she knew more about what was happening in Mexico than any other North American. Tall, blonde shoulder-length hair, in a navy blue silk suit, she stood out in this crowd, as she would in any crowd.

"I've just heard that Brazil and Argentina are defaulting too," she said, getting out the little spiral note pad that reporters always carry. "Can you confirm that? Do you think the dominoes are beginning to topple?"

"I can't confirm it, Mary. But, I wouldn't be surprised, would you?"

"No, I wouldn't," she said, scribbling in her notebook. "That will be the ball game, won't it?"

I said, "It looks very serious to me," and kept walking, tempted as I was not to. The TV crews had moved to the lobby and were trying to get footage of the crowd, and trying to interview anyone they could; but everyone seemed to be going someplace, in a hurry. I wondered if they were going to call their brokers.

As I made my way to the front door, I noticed one person who didn't seem to be in a hurry. Sitting in a lounge chair reading a newspaper was the Mexican I had first seen on the plane.

XIV

I managed to get back across the street to the embassy and, not knowing what else to do, went up to Mitchell's office. He was there looking as if he had lost control of everything. He had, it turned out.

He said, "I'm supposed to tell you to report to the conference room, professor. The same one where we were yesterday. The lunch has been canceled but I'm supposed to try and get some food in there. Would you like ham and swiss or roast beef with horseradish?"

"Perhaps an enchilada would be more appropriate for the occasion," I said, as I walked out of his office wondering where there might be a private telephone I could use.

Someone had put a bank of telephones in the conference room, but Moelker was already there and talking on one of them. He motioned to me to come on in.

"But, Al," he said into the phone, "that's ridiculous. You can't just close the doors of one of the biggest banks in the world."

It must be Albert Collins the president of Chase Manhattan, I thought to myself. This was another one of those days I was glad I had decided not to be a banker.

"I don't care what your people think. Can't you just wait a little while, until I can get back to you?"

There was a pause. Moelker was shaking his head and looking as if he was about to swallow his cigar, or the stub that was left of it. I figured someday he would.

'Well, okay," he said, "Do whatever you think you have to, but I don't like it, and . . . Al, I'm not going to forget this. I'll be back to you as soon as I see the president."

He slammed the receiver down and said, "Jesus, the whole thing is falling apart. That was Collins, and he says they're going to close the bank. He says the market is going crazy, and he thinks they are going to suspend trading any minute. People are beginning to line up at the banks wanting their money. It looks like a full-fledged run."

"Jesus," I said, just now remembering that I had my own account at that bank. "What about the others?"

"From what I can find out, Citicorp, Manny Hanny, Bank of America . . . all of them are closing. Damn, I can't believe it!" He picked up the phone again, and said, "I've got to talk to the rest of them," as he was dialing.

This clearly wasn't the place for me to make a call so I said, "I'll be back in a minute," and left him to the phone. I didn't know what had happened to the president and Lacy, but this seemed like a good time to check out a couple of things. In the middle of the excitement I had almost forgotten about Los Palos.

I went back to Mitchell's office and asked his secretary if there was a private phone I could use. There was, just down the hall, in a legal attaché's office who was out-of-town, or something. I took out my little address book and looked up Jim Halerpin, my friend at the CIA. The lines were all busy and it took three tries to get through, but I finally did.

"Hello, Jim. Cameron Mitchell. I'm in Mexico City and all hell has broken loose. Is there anything I need to know?"

"God, Cam. I'm glad you called. I've been trying to get hold of you, but they say you were at the conference. I was just getting ready to have someone track you down."

"So what's up?" I asked, now beginning to wonder.

"Well, there are some things you need to know. We're almost sure that your friend Cordes was killed by someone from Mexico. Someone who, we think, is connected with a neo-Nazi organization called Los Palos. They're based in Guadalajara."

"Yes, I know," I said. And I quickly told him about my meeting with José Muñoz.

"Does Kral know about this?" he asked.

"Yes, he does. I told him this morning. Also Lacy and the president."

"Good," he said, seemingly relieved. "It looks like we've got a real problem on our hands. Let me check around some more and get back to you."

"Okay Jim. Thanks. And . . . Jim? I've got one more question. I have this feeling that I'm being followed. There's a Mexican—sunglasses, moustache—who seems to be showing up everywhere I go. If it weren't for him I think I might have been hit by a cab at the airport. He pulled me out of the way. Maybe it's just a coincidence, but I've seen him twice since then . . ."

"You must mean Felipe. He's one of our people, just keeping an eye on you. I didn't say anything before because I didn't want you to worry. We put him in after you called me the first time. After what you told me about Cordes I thought you might need someone to keep an eye on you."

"Felipe? Jesus, he had me convinced he was a former bracero. He told me he used to pick artichokes in Watsonville."

"Well," Halerpin said, "he's been around. We had some trouble with the farm workers once."

"I guess he has," I said, finding all this hard to believe. I should have known better. "Well, I guess you know what you are doing. Thanks, Jim. I appreciate it. But Jim . . . it's not Felipe I'm talking about. This guy looks like a businessman, well-dressed. He seems to be everywhere I go. I just saw him in the hotel lobby a few minutes ago."

"Well that doesn't compute at all. Let me check it out, and you'd better tell Kral about it."

"Okay, I will. And, Jim? One other thing. I wonder if you shouldn't have someone look out for Muñoz. He's going to be important to us if this thing comes down. And besides, he's a good friend of mine."

"You may be right, Cam. I'll see what I can do."

"Thanks, Jim."

XV

If I was going to call Ann, this was my chance. I dialed. Busy. All international lines busy, the operator said. When the international lines are busy you just keep dialing. I did. Again, and again . . . finally . . . "Hello?"

"Hi, hon. Thought maybe I'd better check in. Things are crazy here and this is the first time I've had time to get to a phone."

"Cam! I'm so glad you called. It's on the TV, on all of the networks. What's happening? I was just downtown and it looks like everybody in town is standing around in front of the bank, and it's closed. I tried to cash a check at the grocery store, and they wouldn't take it. Dan Rather says it looks like 1933 again. What should I do?"

"Listen, Annie, there's no reason to panic. Just keep calm."

"But what's going to happen?"

"I don't know, hon, I just don't know. But there's nothing we can do about it now. So just listen. I don't have much time. You know the safe in my study . . . don't you?"

"Of course."

"Well, there's some money in there, in a yellow envelope. Take whatever you need and stock up on groceries. And you'd better get both cars filled up with gas. Also . . ."

Mitchell was at the door. "Professor? The president wants you in the conference room now."

"Okay, I'll be right there," I said partly into the receiver, so Ann could hear. "Look, hon, I've got to go. Just get some supplies in and keep an eye on the TV. I'll try to call you again as soon as I can."

"All right, I will, but this has really got me worried. When are you coming back? Do you want me to pick you up at the airport?"

"I don't know yet, hon, but I'll be back as soon as I can. I've got to go."

"Cam?"

"Yeah."

"I love you."

"Me too. I love you too, hon. We'll see ya soon. You hang in there. Bye, bye."

As I started down the hall toward the conference room, Kral shouted out at me from Mitchell's office. "Hey, professor, wait a minute."

"What's up?" I said as soon as I got to the door.

"Come on in. And close the door please, if you don't mind," he said in a voice that didn't sound at all like the confident military man I had seen this morning. He looked me in the eye and said, "José Muñoz has been killed."

God, I'd been right, but too late. I should have known. There's a protective shield that comes over your mind when something like this happens. At first you don't believe it, and you react instinctively, thinking that there is something you can do. But there isn't. It's only later that the reality sinks in and you cry, or at least try to. All I could think of to say was, "When?" Which sounded stupid when I said it.

"Just this morning. He was shot point-blank as he was getting into his car to go to work. It looks like there were two men with machine guns. They apparently got over the wall, killed the dog, and hid in the car. When he opened the door, that was it. There's no trace of them, no fingerprints, nothing. They just disappeared, in broad daylight."

"God. Los Palos."

"I'm afraid so, professor. We're checking it out, but it looks like you were right. He's the first person they would try to take out. We don't even want to think about who the second person might be."

I knew but I had to ask anyway. "Me, I suppose?"

"That's my best guess, Cameron. I think you'd better stay in the embassy until things calm down a bit."

"Well, there's something I need to tell you." And I started to tell him about my conversation with Halerpin, but he stopped me.

"I know," he said. "We'd better get to the meeting. The president is waiting."

XVI

Dawson, Lacy, Hammett, and Moelker were sitting at the conference table eating their sandwiches in silence. Seldom have I seen anyone so intent on lunch. The president motioned for us to have one. There was a platter of ham and roast beef sandwiches. I took a beef on rye, and poured myself some coffee. It looked as though Mitchell had come through.

Talking with his mouth full of ham and swiss the president said, "Well, gentlemen, this is it. From what I can tell everything is falling apart back home. The banks are closed. The market has suspended trading, and the TV boys are playing it up big. And here I am in Mexico.

"I've got Mitchell setting up a satellite feed in case we decide that I should go on TV. So, if I do, what the hell am I supposed to say, 'Oh, don't worry, everything is fine?' Let's have some goddamned ideas fellas, and make it quick. Is there anything new?"

"Well, sir," Kral said. "We've just found out that Muñoz has been killed. He was the . . ."

"Steve," the President interrupted, "I know who he is, ah, I mean, I guess I should say, who he was. So, what does that mean? Who in the hell did it?"

"My best guess is that it was Los Palos," Kral said.

"So now we know this is no joke," the president said.

Then turning to me, "I'm very sorry to hear that, Cam. He was a friend of yours, wasn't he?"

"Yes, he was. I first met him when I was teaching here, a long time ago. He was a good man and a damn good economist."

"Steve," the president said, "what have you found out about these Palos?"

"Well, nothing new yet, except that the Mexican Secret Service has apparently been keeping them under surveillance for quite a while now. And the Mexicans seem to want to cooperate with us. So I should have some more on it soon."

The president said, "Well, keep after it. So, now what are we going to do? Doesn't anybody have any frigging ideas?"

"Could I say something, sir?," I asked.

"Please do. Go ahead."

"Well, I think we should buy it out."

"What do you mean 'buy it out'?" Lacy asked.

"Well," I said, "look, there are three different things going on here. Mexico is bankrupt. So is the rest of Latin America. Our banks are about to go bankrupt and, if that happens the international financial system will collapse, not to mention our own economy. So, obviously, something has to be done to put a stop to it. What it costs is irrelevant compared to the other consequences."

"And so?" the president said.

"So I propose that the Federal Reserve, in cooperation with the Treasury and the IMF simply guarantee all Mexican governmental loans that have been made by U.S. banks."

"Out of the one hundred billion the Mexicans owe, or owed, I should say, seventy-five billion is governmental.

Twenty-five billion of that is owed to our banks. So, if we just guaranteed only the interest on that part of their debt, that would take the banks off the hook. It would only cost around . . ." I took out the little pocket calculator I always carry " . . .two billion, maybe less if interest rates stay down." And I glanced at Moelker and smiled.

"Well, shit!" the president said, "Let's do it. Two billion dollars is nothing."

"Now wait just a goddamn minute here," Moelker said, his face getting red. "The Federal Reserve doesn't guarantee private bank loans. If we started doing that we might just as well nationalize the whole U.S. banking system."

"What," I asked, "did you do in the Continental Illinois case? They were bankrupt and you bailed them out."

"Well, that's different; besides guaranteeing the loans just for our banks is not going to solve the problem. What about the other seventy-five billion?"

"The rest," I said, "is spread out among the European, Japanese, and Arab banks, and the IMF, the World Bank and the Inter-American Development Bank. Since we control the international banks we could get them to cooperate. Then we would just have to convince the others that it's in their best interest to go along. After today that shouldn't be too hard. They don't want to see the system collapse any more than we do. I'll bet you even money on that."

"But," Hammett said, "isn't that just rewarding the banks for their own stupidity? They should never have gotten themselves in this mess in the first place. I really don't like the idea of the government bailin' out the banks every time we turn around."

"Well," I said, "you wouldn't have to guarantee it at

market interest rates. If you set the guarantee at, say, a percentage point below the London interbank rate then they would still take a loss, but they wouldn't have to write off the loans as nonperforming. So they wouldn't, technically at least, be bankrupt. They would still be in business and they could open their doors again. That would stop the run. Also we wouldn't be guaranteeing the private loans so they would still take some losses there."

"So," the president said, "it's like giving them a slap on the hand instead of a kick in the ass?"

"That," I said, "is my perception."

"So," Moelker said, "you're suggesting that we just start guaranteeing all foreign loans from now on? That's ridiculous."

"Well, doesn't the Export-Import bank guarantee export loans every day?" I asked. "And doesn't the FDIC guarantee bank deposits?"

"Yeah, sure," Moelker replied, "but that's different."

"How," the president asked, "is it different?"

"Well, ah . . ." Moelker started to reply when I interrupted. I had learned long ago that when things start to heat up in a discussion like this, the subtle art of interrupting is the key to winning arguments. That's why people with loud voices usually win out. They just talk right over you.

So I said, "Can I talk?" Joan Rivers would have been proud. "Look, there is no reason the guarantee arrangement has to be permanent. We simply guarantee all loans up to the present. Then we propose to Córdoba that we consider this to be a twenty-year moratorium on payments to creditors. It would, in essence, be just like a Chapter Eleven bankruptcy.

"Then the Mexicans have time to get their economy in order, and to restructure their export sector so that they are not so dependent on oil. In twenty years we'll be running out of oil and oil prices will be back up again anyway, and without the drag of the loans their economy is not in such bad shape any way you look at it. It will be a long time, I would bet, before they do any more borrowing from anyone."

"Also with the right kind of encouragement from us, the IMF, the World Bank, and the IADB could put some growth-oriented money in there on a low-interest, long-term basis; and the whole thing would probably come back into balance. No one loses, everybody gains, and we're not staring at a collapse of the international monetary system and a worldwide depression."

"I'll buy it," the president said. "Robert?"

"Well, okay, but I don't like it."

"Hugh?"

"Count me in," Hammett said.

"So, what do we have to do now?" Dawson said, looking at Lacy. When it came to actually doing anything, it always seemed to be Lacy who did it.

"Well," Lacy said, "I guess we have to get Córdoba to go along. And we have to take care of this Palos thing. Steve, can you handle that?"

"Consider it done," Kral said.

"Good. Then I think maybe it's time for Cameron to have another informal chat with our friend Córdoba. I'll set it up right away. Okay, Cam?"

"No problem," I said. "No problem at all."

"That could be dangerous," Kral said. "We don't know what these Palos may be up to. Let's don't forget what happened to Muñoz."

"Well, I've always got Felipe," I said.
"Who in the hell is Felipe?" the president asked.
"My cab driver."

XVII

"I think, professor, if you don't mind, that we might take the scenic route today," Felipe said as he U-turned the cab in the opposite direction from Los Pinos, toward Chapultepec Park.

"I'm with you, Felipe," I said, surprised but realizing the logic of his argument. We turned right at the park, passed some of the palatial mansions where most of the Mexican government officials—and the U.S. ambassador—lived, and dropped quickly into real Mexico, the *barrio*. Children were playing in the streets, seemingly oblivious to the squalor amid some starving dogs, assorted street vendors and shoeshine boys standing around. Even with Felipe laying on the horn constantly it was slow going.

Blocked at an intersection we watched as a young man came out of nowhere, stood in front of the cab, took a drink of something out of an old Coca-Cola bottle, held a match to his mouth and belched out a torrent of flame. Then he came to the window and held out his hand. He expected to be paid for the show.

"The fire-eaters," Felipe said as he inched the cab ahead ignoring the circus act. "They slowly absorb the kerosene and die. Gives you an idea of what this place is coming to." I couldn't think of any logical response.

We were blocked again, this time by a truck full of chickens apparently being delivered somewhere by someone who was nowhere in sight. A uniformed policeman appeared. Without comment Felipe handed him a 500-peso bill and he went chasing into a nearby small street store looking for the truck driver who promptly materialized and moved the truck so we could pass.

"What do the police make these days?" I asked, just curious.

"A street patrol like him? About thirty dollars a week if he's lucky. Plus maybe another thirty in tips for letting people park, less the ten he has to pay his boss for letting him keep the job. If he knows how to drive, which he probably doesn't, and could get together a couple hundred dollars he could maybe buy a job driving a patrol car. That pays better because the bribes are higher. A traffic ticket costs me two dollars these days, but sometimes I talk them out of it by just arguing with them and taking a lot of their time. Sometimes I just pay, depending on if I'm in a hurry or not. It's the motorcycle guys you have to watch out for, they've got a cousin or a brother somewhere high up and they carry real guns. Get stopped by one of them and it's going to cost you ten or fifteen depending on how their day has been going. Usually, though, they don't bother the taxis these days. They know we don't have any money, I guess. Who knows?"

We were still inching along and as I was beginning to wonder how long it was going to take us to get to Los Pinos I heard a heavy thud sound. The windshield splattered. At first I thought a kid had thrown a rock or something at us. I looked around not sure what to do. In front of the cab in broad daylight were two well-dressed Mexicans with Israeli Uzis—the professionals' weapon of choice—trained directly on us. Then more THUD THUD THUD. The windows cracked but didn't break—bulletproof, I should have known. I glanced to the right and saw another Uzi pointed right at my face.

The street people were doing everything possible to make themselves invisible, crawling under parked cars and running somewhere fast. The gunmen were oblivious to them.

"Get down, professor. Down on the floor!" Felipe yelled as he gunned the car foward into an intersection. The last thing I saw was a black van pulling in front of us blocking the way. Felipe swung sharply to the right trying to avoid it. He didn't. We bounced off. Another THUD as we crashed into a corner building. My head hit the front seat, and that was the last THUD of the day for me. It was enough for one day.

XVIII

When I woke up—if that's what you could call it—my head felt as if it were bigger than it should be. I felt it. It was. My right arm and shoulder were bruised and swollen and I could barely move my hand. My back was crying out for a chiropractor. I was in pajamas. My own. A hospital, I must be in a hospital, was my first thought as my eyes and my mind began to slowly come into focus. How else could I be in my own all-cotton flannel pajamas?

I lay still for a while thinking that if I just went back to sleep this would all turn out to be a bad dream. Maybe I fell out of bed. That would explain why the whole right side of my body was telling me something was very wrong. But I kept hearing this THUD. Not the kind of thud you have when you have a hangover, but the kind of thud most people never hear. The thud of a bullet bouncing off of bulletproof glass. It's not a splat, like in the movies, but a THUD. Just a plain old thud.

Then I woke up, for sure this time. Felipe. The cab. Los Pinos. Córdoba. Well-dressed Mexicans with Uzis. The van. The crash. I was, I finally decided, lucky to be alive. Los Palos. Gómez-Hil. A coup. DEFAULT!

So now the question became: Where was I? I inched my way out of the bed. I couldn't move my right arm, but my legs seemed okay. I sat on the edge of the bed and tried to take stock of what, I was beginning to realize, was not the best of all possible situations. The room seemed to be a normal bedroom, a guest room perhaps. A bed, a couple of uncomfortable looking chairs, a bathroom, and a closet. There was a window covered with the wooden shutters that most upper-class Mexican houses have. Some light was seeping in, so it must still be daytime. What day, I didn't know.

I splashed some cold water in my face and wondered if I could negotiate the shower. I couldn't, I decided. I opened the closet and there hanging neatly were my clothes. *All* my clothes and my suitcase. And on the floor next to it was my briefcase, just sitting there looking like it was ready to go out for a day's work. My mind said I should look to see what was still in it. My back said I shouldn't. I didn't. Instead I managed to get some clothes on.

I worked my way to the window, opened the shutters. Just a normal window, no glass and no screens, just steel bars, vertical about six inches apart. The question now became: Were they to keep me in, or to keep other people out? Bars on windows are not uncommon in Mexico. But, whatever their original purpose, it was clear enough they would do a pretty good job of keeping me in.

Beyond the bars I could see an expansive manicured lawn-garden. The grass golf-course-green green. It was fenced on two sides with high hedges and bougainvilleas in bloom, red and white. It sloped down to a narrow white sand beach. Two power boats were tied to a small dock, one a Cigarette, the speedboat Florida dope smugglers use. Beyond that far out in what seemed to be a large lake was an island topped by a large statue. And beyond that the orange setting sun reflecting on the tranquil lake. It was almost dusk, but I could just make out fishermen in small canoes with large kitelike nets skimming the smooth lake surface like drowning butterflies.

The butterfly fishermen jarred me back to reality. Pátzquaro! I was in a house on Lake Pátzquaro, in the middle of Mexico, the mountain lake I had visited many times with Ann, Becky, and José. The Indian fishermen lived on the island and made their living netting the famed Pátzquaro whitefish. The statue of Hildago watched over them. The sun was setting over the island so I must be on the east side of the lake, the isolated side, far from curious tourists. Or anybody. Except Los Palos.

I looked around the room again, trying to decide what to do next and realized that I had completely forgotten about the door. I edged over to it and tried the knob. It was, as I had assumed, locked. I studied it briefly to see if I could maybe take the hinges off or something. There weren't any hinges. They must be on the outside. The door was solid oak. Out of frustration I suppose more than anything I kicked it a few times. Outside I heard muffled voices and someone walking somewhere.

"Well, hotshot professor," I said out loud to myself, "I guess it's time to reassess your situation." My head throbbed relentlessly and my right arm hurt, but I was now able to move my fingers—a little. In the assortment of pills I always carry with me were some Advils, if they were still in my briefcase maybe a couple would help. I couldn't stoop over but I squatted down gingerly and picked up the briefcase, laid it on the bed and opened it. The pills were there, but the briefing papers and the letter from José were gone. Not that I was surprised.

I got out a couple of Advils and worked my way back to the bathroom now pondering the ridiculousness of having to decide whether or not to drink the water. I decided not, amoebic dysentery was not what I needed right now, and choked down the Advils dry. It wasn't easy.

The problem of what to do next was decided for me when someone unlocked and opened the door without knocking. My Mexican friend and shadow from the plane walked in casually, smiled, and said, "Well, professor, how are you feeling today?" like we were old friends. Behind him was another well-dressed Mexican carrying a black bag.

"I've had better days," I said. "Would you mind telling me what in the hell is going on?"

"You'll find out soon enough, professor, but right now I want the Doctor to take a look at you. This is Dr. González." And with that he sat down in the chair and lit a cigarette.

The doctor, who looked to be about twenty-five years old, said, "Please lie down on the bed, sir, and let's have a look at you." He felt around on my head and shoulder and asked, "Can you move your fingers?" I moved them a little to show him I could, not knowing what else to do. He seemed a harmless sort. "Well, I don't think you have any broken bones or a concussion. Tell you what, I'm going to give you a couple of aspirin and I'll check on you again tomorrow. But you had better take it easy for a few days. Okay?"

"I just took two Advils, thanks."

"Okay. Take these later. Take six or eight a day. They will help the pain and keep the inflammation down." He then closed up his little black bag and left as if it were a routine house call. Maybe it was.

After he had gone the Mexican said, "There is someone who wants to see you, professor. You think you can walk okay? Here, let me help you with your coat." And with his help I managed to get it on. Then he pointed to the door. "Let's go," he said in a way that made it clear I didn't have much choice. We walked out into a dimly lit hallway and he helped me down a long flight of stairs.

"Would you mind telling me what's going on?" I asked him again. "Who are you? And why have you been following me?"

"You'll find out soon enough, professor. This way, please," and he steered me down another corridor to a large arched double door. He knocked and opened it at the same time. Then I entered another world.

At first I thought it was a chapel of some kind. The roof was beamed and arched. The windows stained glass: all red. There were no lights; only candles and a few Mexican paper lanterns provided dim light. It was like walking into a dark movie theater. At first I couldn't see anything, but then my eyes began to adjust. That seemed a mixed blessing.

There were churchlike pews on each side of an aisle that led to what appeared to be an altar. Seated behind a long oak table were three men—dressed in black monk's robes. Behind them, dominating the decor, was a large Nazi flag—the symbol of the Third Reich. And on each side of that were two crosses—the symbol of the crucifixion. Whatever all that meant I didn't know, but whatever it was it was obvious that this wasn't going to be one of my better days.

My Mexican guide motioned for me to sit down on one of the hardwood chairs lined up in front of the imposing table. With some effort I did, and he sat down in one of the pews behind me.

The black-robed monks—or whatever they were—were studying some papers and chatting in Spanish, ignoring me. I had a fleeting memory of the time when, as a Ph.D. candidate, I sat for my oral examination. The monk on my left looked up at me through horn-rimmed glasses, pulled back his hood and said, "Well, professor, it's good to see you again."

It was Manuel Gómez-Hil.

"I'm sorry you got banged up. It wouldn't have happened if that driver of yours hadn't tried to get away. But they tell me you'll be okay."

Felipe. Jesus, I had forgotten all about Felipe. "Where is he? Is he okay?" I asked, trying to pull myself together, but doubting that it was going to matter much.

"Your CIA friend?" Gómez-Hil said, "I'm sure he's being taken care of."

"Would you mind telling me what's going on here. Where are we, and what do you think you're doing? Don't you know that the entire U.S. Army is going to be looking for me by now. Kidnapping is a serious offense."

"There's no need to be alarmed, professor," Gómez-Hil said. "You'll be released in due time. We just need to

106

keep you out of the way for a few days. Then you can go home. In any case, there's someone here who wants to talk to you," and he motioned to the Mexican sitting in the pew behind me. The other two monks hadn't said a word. They just stared at me.

The Mexican got up and walked back up the aisle and out the door. "So you're a Palo," I said to Gómez-Hil.

"That much, professor, you've got figured out. But you don't understand," he said, as a side door opened and someone came in. In the dim light I couldn't see who it was, but the monks all stood up and said in unison: "Sieg Heil!" as they raised their arms in the traditional Nazi salute.

"Hello, Cameron," Jim Halerpin said to me, ignoring the monks. "Nice to see you."

XIX

I hadn't seen Halerpin for a while and he looked heavier than I had remembered. He wore a crew cut, a black suit, and black tie. White shirt. "What in the hell are you doing here"? I asked, my mind a total blank. I felt like I had just run into my priest in a whorehouse.

"Well, professor, there are a few things you don't understand."

"That would seem to be a bit of an understatement," I said, regaining my composure, and beginning to realize that things were getting much more complicated than I had thought. Here I am in the middle of Mexico looking at three men dressed like the grim reaper and talking to an old friend who is a highly placed CIA official who I had just talked to on the phone yesterday and he's saying there are a few things I don't understand. I was beginning to realize that I was in some serious trouble. "Maybe you could explain it to me then," I said. "Am I to assume you are a Palo?"

"That would be a fair assumption," he said. It was then that I realized that my chances of getting out of here were somewhere between "slim" and "none." If I knew that a CIA officer was involved in a neo-Nazi secret organization that was plotting the overthrow of the Mexican government, they surely couldn't just let me go home as if nothing had happened.

"So what do you want with me?" I asked. "I certainly can't do anything for you."

"Well, I think you can, professor," he said, putting one foot on one of the chairs and leaning on his knee. "What you can do is do nothing. That's why we had to bring you here. You are the one person who could possibly stop the default, and we can't allow that to happen. There's too much at stake now."

"But what do you think you can gain from all this, Jim?" I said, deciding that if I got more friendly at least he might talk.

"It's not what we *think* we will gain, it's what we *will* gain," he said, beginning to pace up and down in front of the table. The others were just staring at me, expressionless. "Within a few days we will have control of the international monetary system and, with that, control of the Western world."

"You're crazy, Jim. You of all people know Dawson will never let a coup happen in Mexico. They'll have the army in here before you know what happened. They are already on alert."

"I know, but you see, shortly the Army is going to be

a bit preoccupied. We have some plans for them. One well-placed explosion in each of the major U.S. cities will cause the system to collapse—temporarily at least. Long enough for us to do what we want to do." He was talking as calmly as if we were discussing yesterday's football scores. "You see, my friend, we are but part of a worldwide organization of people devoted to restoring order to the world. We have people in every major country in the world. The coup in Mexico will be but the beginning of a very complicated domino game. Argentina will be next, then Brazil, then Chile. In a very short time we will have control of all of Latin America.

"We have already cut the jugular vein—the banking system. The banks in the States are already closed. They won't be reopening any time soon," and with that he looked at Gómez-Hil and smiled.

"It's the financial system that is the Achilles Heel of the capitalist system. The first mistake was the Bretton Woods Conference. Keynes tried to tell you, remember? He said making the dollar the linchpin of the international financial system would never work. It took longer than we thought it would but we knew he was right. It was just a matter of time, and the time is now.

"You were just too greedy!" he went on, his voice gathering emotion. "Did you think the world was just going to stand by and let you suck up its resources on an unlimited line of credit? Did you think the world was going to continue financing your deficits so you could live like kings and queens in a sea of starvation?"

"Well, I guess . . ." I started to say but he interrupted me.

"How interesting it is, professor, that it was the banks themselves who caused their own demise and what will now be the end of the system. The end of capitalism. Loaning a trillion dollars to the Third World and expecting them to repay it by transferring all of their resources to you was the epitome of stupid greed. And it was the final link, professor; it fell right into our hands. Now we will take over. The Third Reich will rise again!"

Then the monks all stood up. "Sieg Heil!" they said in unison, raising their arms in salute. There wasn't anything for me to say that would make any sense. I knew enough to realize that when you are talking to a lunatic you have to accept his logic. I had tried to argue with the John Birchers enough to know that. So I asked, "And what, may I ask, does all this have to do with me?"

"We will need you, professor, when the time comes to put a new international financial system in place. We need people like you, who understand the system. I am hoping you will cooperate. That, by the way, is why your life was spared. That and the fact that I have always liked you, even if you are a bit naive."

"And if I don't cooperate?"

"You will, when you understand what we plan to do. But, for now I'll have to ask you to stay with us for a while. You always liked Lake Pátzquaro, didn't you?" Halerpin motioned to the Mexican who had been sitting silently behind me, and he escorted me out and back to the bedroom that was apparently going to be my prison cell.

As we entered the room, I said, "Do you think you could find me something to read? Isn't there a copy of *Mein Kampf* or something around here?"

"I'll see what I can find, professor. Maybe I can bring something around later tonight." Then he put one finger over his lips in the "shush . . ." sign and handed me a small piece of paper. On it was written.

FLUSH THIS DOWN THE TOILET. STAY AWAKE TONIGHT.

He said, "Well, you'd better get some rest, professor. Someone will be around with some food for you soon." And he left.

XX

I lay down on the bed and stared at the ceiling. My head was numb, my arm throbbed, and my mind was telling me to go to sleep. But the Mexican was telling me to stay awake. What in the hell did that mean? I had to get this sorted out. He was telling me to stay awake and didn't want to say it out loud. That had to mean the room was bugged, which didn't surprise me. But if he was passing me a note and telling me to flush it down the toilet that had to mean he wasn't what he appeared to be.

But he'd been following me since I had left Denville, and he probably saved me from being run down by a cab at the airport. Part of that seemed to add up to him being a Palo henchman, or even a hit man if he was the one who killed Arturo, but part of it didn't add up at all.

That left me with the question of whether or not I could or should trust him. My mind said no, but the economist in me was reminding me that you have to make decisions based on the best knowledge you have available at the time, and that your decisions are only as good as the assumptions you make. Once the assumptions are made it's just a question of following through the logic until you have the solution. Flawed as it may be, you have to act on it, or not act at all. Since I didn't have any verifiable information that he was, in fact, a Palo—except that he was here, and obviously trusted by them—I decided to go along with whatever he was up to. Besides, what alternatives did I have? I struggled to keep awake, but it was a losing cause. I dozed off.

I woke with a start as I heard someone saying, "Professor! Come on, we're going to get you out of here." Someone was outside the window prying the bars open with a large crowbar. It was the Mexican. "Let's see if you can squeeze through here now," he said in a low voice. "Stand on the chair. Then see if you can step through."

I quickly considered my alternatives again. There weren't any, except to go along with whatever it was that was happening to me now. Whatever happened was going to be interesting, that much was obvious. "Okay, I'll try," I said, "but it looks a little tight." The opening looked to be about eighteen inches at the widest point.

"Stand on the ledge, and put your feet through first. Then I'll pull you out. And hurry."

"Okay, here goes," I said, as I held on to the bars and half swung and half fell out. I was beginning to appreciate the logistical complexities of being a breech baby. It wasn't as hard to squeeze a thirty-eight-inch waist through an eighteen-inch hole as I had imagined and I somehow found myself standing in a flower bed wondering if any of my ribs were broken.

"Follow me," he said as he motioned toward the water and started off at a half trot toward the hedge then down to the lakeshore beach. The moon reflected some gray light, and as my eyes adjusted to the darkness I realized we were heading toward the dock. The only thing he said was, "keep following me and don't look back. We're going to take a little boat ride."

It was then that I realized he was carrying an Uzi. He hopped onto the dock and then up the small ladder onto the Cigarette, the sleek and powerful racing boat. They're capable, I remembered from somewhere, of speeds up to ninety miles an hour. He turned and helped me on board and said, "Get in that seat and keep your head down." And with that he started the powerful engines and backed us out. Slowly at first we headed out toward the island. "Now stand up, professor, and hold on to that railing." He pushed the throttle forward and almost instantly we were, it seemed, literally flying over the water in a surge of acceleration that reminded me of the feeling you have when a jet accelerates toward takeoff speed. There is a point on takeoff when the plane is committed to fly. We had, I suspected, reached that point. The point of no return.

"Bend your knees, professor, otherwise the vibration will break your back," the Mexican yelled at me over the deafening roar, "and hang on." I did, deciding that motorboat racing was one sport I could easily get along without if the option ever came up. Certainly it wasn't a sport for people with false teeth. The noise made it impossible for me to ask the same question I had been asking all day: "Would you mind telling me what in the hell is going on here?" A couple minutes more of vibration torture. Then we veered right around the island. Now behind it the Mexican decelerated and we were cruising along like a couple of playboys out for an evening joyride. The Mexican looked at me, smiled, and said, "We're okay, I think. They don't have anything that can catch us now."

"So now, would you mind telling me what's going on?" I asked.

"You'll find out soon enough, professor. Right now we've got to concentrate on getting you out of here."

"Then can you at least tell me where we're going?"

"Back to Mexico City," he said.

He throttled down again and eased us into a cove and up to a small dock. The silver moonlight illuminated the lake and wooded shore. There was no sound but the dull throb of our engines and the lap of the gentle waves licking at the small beach, and no lights anywhere. The cove was totally secluded.

"Come on, follow me, professor. Now we're going to take a little hike," he said as he hopped over the side and held out his hand to help me down the ladder to the dock. It was the first time I remembered that I could barely move my right arm and my ribs felt as if I had just quarterbacked the Super Bowl. But my mind kept telling me this was a good time to keep moving. So I stumbled along the uphill path through the woods following my enigmatic Mexican guide.

Ten minutes more of torture and we were at the top of what I now realized was almost a cliff. Quickly looking back I could see the island, the statue of Hildago calmly watching over the still lake. Beyond that on the far side of the lake were the twinkling lights of the sleeping village of Pátzquaro. We took another path to the right until we came to a dirt road. There, as if it was waiting for a fare, was a taxicab. Before I had time to contemplate the absurdity of the situation, the Mexican opened the back door and said, "Get in, professor." In the driver's seat was Felipe, his head bandaged, but otherwise looking his normal nonchalant self. The Mexican got in behind me and shut the door quietly.

"Where to Señores?" Felipe said, smiling, as we surged ahead, the lights off. I started to say something but the Mexican interrupted me talking to Felipe in the rapid slanglike Spanish that no one but a native speaker can understand. All I could make out was "radio."

Felipe picked up the handset below the dashboard and was barking commands into the static. All I could get out of that was "listo" and "ahorita"—ready, right now. We bounced along in the dark for a few more minutes and then Felipe pulled the cab up abruptly under a tree on the edge of a clearing. It was, I realized, a landing strip. Someone was running along in the darkness with a torch, lighting other torches, which were apparently to serve as landing lights. Felipe said, pointing to the sky, "Your flight will be in any minute now, professor."

Above the profile of the mountains I could see the familiar landing lights of a plane on final approach. In the setting it could just as well have been a flying saucer. It swooped past us, jet engines screaming in reverse as the pilot struggled to stop the plane on the short runway. It was a Lear Jet. Felipe gunned the cab forward and we were now following the plane to the far end of the strip. The pilot swung the jet around and we pulled up alongside. The noise of the engines was deafening. The door opened and the stairs fell out. Then two men with rifles dressed in black jumped out and stood on each side of the stairs. Felipe jumped out of the cab and opened the door on my side and said, "Let's go, professor!"

I didn't have to be encouraged. We quickly scrambled abroad and the Mexican followed, then the two men dressed in black. Before we even had time to sit down the plane was screaming down the runway. I braced myself and then half fell into a seat. I instinctively thought of the seat belt but none of that made any sense, so I just concentrated on staying in the seat. Felipe and the others were doing the same.

In a matter of seconds we were in the air and climbing rapidly as we banked sharply to the left. When we reached cruising altitude, the pilot switched on the cabin lights and Felipe got up and said, "Would you like a drink, professor? And a sandwich perhaps? We've got about a thirty-minute flight to Mexico City."

Then I realized that I hadn't eaten all day. Eating wasn't something I often forgot. "Please, Felipe," I said, "anything you've got would be fine."

Felipe opened a small bar and pulled out a bottle of Tangueray and proceeded to mix us all a martini. "Olive?"

"Four please, and make it a double, if you don't mind, on the rocks," I said.

"No problem," he said as he handed the two men in black a couple of Carta Blanca beers and said something to them in Spanish. They smiled, nodded, and disappeared through the small forward door toward the cockpit. The cabin was standard executive-jet issue. Tastefully appointed with four comfortable swivel-seat chairs, a small fold-down table, bar, and small refrigerator. Felipe mixed our drinks and one for himself and handed them and a sandwich from the fridge to each of us. Then he pulled down the folding table and we all swiveled the chairs around so that we were all just sitting there having a drink and a snack as though we were in a corner bar. I decided that asking what was going on was getting a bit redundant, so instead I inhaled the ham and swiss and the martini. I was gaining a new appreciation for ham and swiss sandwiches.

"Well, professor, I suppose you are wondering what's going on?" Felipe said.

"You could say that," I said.

"Let me introduce you to Rafael Zarate of the Mexican Servicio Secreto, intelligence division."

My now longtime Mexican guide-friend put his hand out and we shook hands. He smiled and said, "My pleasure, professor. I'm sorry about what you had to go through but it couldn't be helped. We made a minor mistake when you got hurt in the wreck. That wasn't in the plan. I hope you'll be all right."

"I'll be okay," I said. "At least I'm alive. That's something. But what I don't understand is how you can be a Mexican Secret Service agent and a Palo at the same time. I had decided you were one of the bad guys."

"Well, I was and I wasn't, I guess you could say. I've been working, how do you say? Undercover . . . ? for Los Palos for several years now. I am, or was, their head of security."

"You were like a mole?"

"Ah, yes, that's it," he said, "a mole."

"You see," Felipe said, "there are people in the Mexican government and in our government who have been interested in Los Palos for a long time now. So we arranged for Rafael to infiltrate them. Eventually he was convincing enough to gain their trust. Once he accomplished that we pretty much knew what they were up to."

"But," I said, "I didn't have the impression Kral knew about that. He doesn't seem very informed about Los Palos?"

"There are a lot of things Kral doesn't know about," Felipe said. "He's a political appointee—they come and go with each new president. Deep undercover operations are run by the career professionals. The director and the president are informed only on a need-to-know basis. You should know that, professor. There are too many leaks coming out of the White House for the president to know everything. Besides, no one person could ever keep track of it all, even if they wanted to."

"So," I said to Rafael, "why were you following me? Were you in Denville when Cordes was killed? I was beginning to think you were the one who killed him."

"That's what I was sent to do, but I didn't get there in time. Halerpin had somehow—I don't know how—found out that Muñoz had sent Cordes to see you. I was dispatched to take care of him and to keep an eye on you. But I didn't get there in time and someone else did the job. I suspect Halerpin had it done or did it himself when he realized there wasn't time for me to intercept Cordes."

I asked, "Would you have killed him?"

"I don't know," Zarate said. "In this world, professor, people are sometimes expendable. It's a matter of statistics. Would you kill one person to save a million?"

"I don't know," I said. It was a problem I hoped I would never have to contemplate seriously.

"So your assignment was to follow me and . . .?"

"And at first to take you out of the picture if it seemed you were going to be able to stop the default. But when you weren't then they wanted to use you if they could. That's why I suggested the kidnapping. I knew I could get you out since they trusted me and we wanted you to see the reality of the situation firsthand. We hadn't planned on Halerpin showing up so soon. That was a lucky bonus. Actually, if Felipe here was a better driver it would have worked out fine. As it was, it worked out."

"You mean to tell me, Felipe, that you knew I was going to be kidnapped when you took the back route through the barrio?" I asked, amazed, but far beyond being surprised at anything by now.

"Sorry about that, boss. But we knew they weren't going to hurt you. They just wanted to take you out of the action for a while, then pick your brains when the time came."

"So, how did you get away?"

"I just played dead. It's an old trick. Besides, it wasn't me they wanted. It was you. And everybody knew the windows were bulletproof, so it was mostly a show to make you feel—shall we say—insecure?"

"Jesus, I must admit you did a good job at that . . . one more thing . . . who killed José Muñoz? Was that really necessary?"

"It was," Rafael said, "one of Gómez-Hil's people. He got on to Muñoz before we had a chance to do anything about it. Each of the Los Palos triad directorate has his own operations. I didn't have much control over that. My job was head of security and special assignments. That's why it was so easy for me to get you out of *la casa*. I had assigned only a couple of guards to you and I just made sure they were sleeping well. But it was too bad. Men like Muñoz are the real heroes of these crazy games."

"And just one more thing, if you don't mind," I said. "What am I supposed to do now?"

"What you have to do, professor, is see President Dawson as soon as we can get you back to the embassy. Now that you've had a firsthand look at things, we hope that you'll be able to explain to him in, shall we say, a more realistic way, what is going on. Then the two of you will have to convince Córdoba to stop the default. After that you fellows can work out the details."

"And what about Gómez-Hil?"

"We . . . ah," Rafael said, "have some plans for him."

"And Halerpin?"

"That's more complicated. But I doubt that Kral and Dawson are going to be too happy to hear . . . from you . . . that one of their top covert section chiefs is engineering a covert plan to take over the world."

"I see what you mean," I said.

XXI

The Lear Jet floated smoothly over the lake bed that is Mexico City, bounced on to the runway of the Mexico City International Airport. We taxied to the left, away from the main terminal. Then to a hangar well away from the bustle of activity that is an airport. One of the men in black, now well-dressed in street clothes, opened the cabin door and signaled for us to follow him. Felipe said, "We have a helicopter waiting, professor. We'll get you to the embassy. After that, you're on your own. Good luck."

"Do they know I'm coming?"

"Everyone who needs to know knows," Felipe said, as we walked toward the helicopter. Zarate was nowhere in sight. In a couple of minutes we were zooming down over the Zona Rosa and then hovering over the American Embassy roof. Red lights turned to green and we were cleared to land.

"So what are you going to do?" I yelled at Felipe over the roar of the chopper engines.

"I'll be around," he said.

I clambered out of the chopper, the wind from the still-swirling rotor blades almost knocking me over. As soon as I was clear the chopper took off again. Off into the night heading who knew where. Standing by the stairs was Lacy.

"Good to see you, professor," he said, stepping forward out of the shadows, "you had us worried for a while there."

"I was a little worried myself, come to think of it," I said, wondering how much he knew. I decided to let him talk. I had to remember I was now dealing with the question of who knew what and who to trust. "So what did you think was going on, when I didn't show up for the meeting with Córdoba?" I asked him.

"Well," he said, as we waited for the elevator, "at first we thought you had been killed in an automobile accident. That was the first report we had from the Mexican police. Then, when that couldn't be verified, we realized that you had probably been kidnapped by Los Palos, or somebody. We had every agent in the country looking for you as well as the Mexican Secret Service, but no one came up with any leads until we got an anonymous call saying that you were coming in by helicopter at around three."

It was, I then realized, almost four in the morning. I had been gone for almost fourteen hours. "So what has happened since I've been gone? Is the president still here?"

"What's happened, my friend, is that every bank in

the country is closed. There have been riots in almost every major city. The White House says there are thousands of people standing around Lafayette Park and all down Pennsylvania Avenue. Then we just heard that there have been bombings at O'Hare, LAX, Dulles, and the Atlanta airports. All flights have been canceled, and the president has declared martial law. The National Guard has been mobilized and all armed forces are on full alert. The entire country is paralyzed. Other than that, there isn't much going on."

"And the president?"

"He's sleeping. But he knows you are back and wants to meet with you, me, and Kral for breakfast at six. So you've got a couple of hours if you want to grab a nap. You look terrible. Do you want me to get a doctor to look at you?"

"No, thanks anyway. I'll be okay, I think. Just find me a couch somewhere."

"Okay, there's one in the conference room next to Mitchell's office," Lacy said, as we got off of the elevator. "But, professor, just tell me one thing. Where have you been? Do you know something we don't?"

"It's a long story, Bill. I've got to think about it. I'll tell you at breakfast." We walked into the conference room and I fell onto the couch. Lacy switched off the light as he left. I thought I was too tired to sleep, but my mind was blank, my body numb. I must have drifted off somehow because I kept seeing myself sitting in the oval office talking with Jim Halerpin. A Nazi flag was prominently displayed behind his desk. Then someone was shaking me.

"Cameron, wake up. You've got to get up." It was

Moelker. I sat straight up, trying to focus my eyes. Coffee was the only thing I could think of. Coffee.

"Is there any coffee around here?" I said, wondering where the bathroom was. There was one at the far end of the room.

As I staggered toward it Moelker said, "I've got some coffee coming." I finished in the bathroom and splashed some water on my face and rinsed the camel-corps taste out of my mouth. Looking at myself in the mirror I realized that I still had on yesterday's shirt, no tie, and that the rest of my clothes were still back at Lake Pátzquaro. I also realized that was the least of my problems. What, I wondered, was Moelker doing here? Certainly if there was a key player in all this it was he. I decided I should confide in him. It would save time when I told the president what had to be done. Moelker's support was crucial. He was sitting at the conference table scribbling something on a yellow pad when I came out. A pot of coffee had appeared from somewhere.

He looked up and said, "Sounds like you've had a busy night."

"You could say that," I said, as I poured myself some coffee. "George, there's something I have to tell you. We've got a real problem here. But, I think the two of us can get it resolved. What's happened is that there's . . ."

"Yes, I know. A renegade CIA section chief who's behind all this. Halerpin, I think his name is. He's behind the Palos and they are the ones who kidnapped you."

"Now, how in the hell did you know that?" I asked, stunned.

"Because someone called me late last night and told me. Also that you would be back soon."

"Who was it?"

"Someone I have every reason to trust."

Then I remembered Felipe's words: "Those who need to know, will know."

"So we've got some work to do," Moelker said. And he handed me the yellow pad. "What I think we can do is buy out the debt, set up a special commission on Third World debt, have it issue bonds, which we will guarantee. Since the debt is trading at only around fifty-seven percent of par in the secondary market right now it won't really cost anybody anything if we act quickly, and the Mexicans and the rest of the debtor countries can have a new start. That way everybody saves face. What do you think?"

"I think it's pretty much what I've been trying to tell you for a long time now."

"Yes, I know," he said. "I know. Do you think Córdoba will buy it?"

"I think Córdoba will buy anything we come up with once I tell him about this whole Palos plot. What we have to do is get him and Dawson to sit down and talk it over. Then once they agree there has to be a joint communiqué. Then you've got to get those banks open again. And somebody has got to take care of Los Palos."

"Okay. That's it. Let's go see Dawson. He's waiting."

XXII

Down the hall and back to the familiar conference room we found the table set for breakfast and Dawson, Kral, and Lacy all looking bleary-eyed. There was a platter of scrambled eggs in the center of the table, bacon, toast, orange juice, and coffee. My stomach said yes.

Dawson hopped up, shook my hand and said, "My God, Cam, it's good to see you. We thought we had lost you." He seemed sincere.

I said, "Well, for a while there I thought you had, too. I think I'd better have some food before we get into this." I was beginning to feel faint, like I might do a nosedive right into the scrambled eggs.

We all started eating and the president said, "Well, gentlemen, unless somebody comes up with a miracle in the next few minutes I'm going to have to get my ass back to Washington. The Air Force fellows say Andrews is still secure for landing and they seem to think they can get me back to the White House. I've got to address the nation, and I'm hoping that by then we'll have some sort of solution to this mess. I talked to the vice-president a few minutes ago and he's about to shit his pants—which is nothing new, but I've got to do something soon, or this shooting match is over. So if anybody has any ideas let's hear them now."

"Sir," I said, "there's something you should know, if you don't already." I glanced at Moelker. He was looking down at the remains of his breakfast.

"And," Dawson said, "that is?"

"I've learned some things that I think would convince Córdoba to change his mind about the default, and we've got a plan about what to do about the default."

"Who is 'we'?" Dawson asked.

"Moelker and I and apparently some people none of us have ever met," I said.

He looked puzzled for a moment, then said, "Go ahead, let's hear it."

"Well, sir, what happened to me yesterday is I was kidnapped by the Palos but rescued by some people who

125

seem to know a lot more about all of this than any of us do." And I quickly recounted the story of Los Palos, Lake Pátzquaro, Jim Halerpin, and the Mexican mole. I left Felipe out of it. Lacy was looking like Orphan Annie, and Kral was ashen. Moelker ceremoniously lit a cigar and was studying the smoke. It was obvious, as I had suspected, that he was the only one who knew. Only those who need to know, Felipe had said.

The president looked at Kral and said, "What the hell is going on here, Steve? You mean to tell me you didn't know about any of this?" He was livid, Kral speechless. "One of your own section chiefs is engineering the overthrow of the Mexican government right under your nose, and someone else in your organization has a mole inside the Palos and you don't even know about it . . . much less I don't? Jesus H. Christ, no wonder things are falling apart."

"Well . . .ah . . . " Kral said, "it's hard to keep track of everything. There's so much going on . . . ah . . . "

"Look, Steve," Dawson said, "would you mind seeing if you can find out what this is all about, or for Chris'sakes, *do something.*"

"Yes, sir," Kral said, with military precision. And he got up and left.

"Now," the president said, "what's this plan?" looking at Moelker and me.

I nodded to Moelker and he briefly laid out the plan: "We'll buy the debt . . . from the banks . . . at market rates . . . set up a commission . . . issue bonds . . . everyone saves face . . ."

"That's enough," Dawson said. "Lacy, get ahold of Córdoba. Tell him we'll be over there at eight. Don't take no for an answer. And get the helicopter ready. And tell Mitchell to find the professor some clean clothes."

"Yes, sir," Lacy said. He sped out of the room and down the hall. Going somewhere.

XXIII

The converted Marine Huey chopper the president uses was a bit more comfortable than the midget I had been on earlier. We edged out of the smog into a clear blue sky, heading for Los Pinos. Dawson, Moelker, and myself, and the ever-present coterie of secret service guards that accompany the president wherever he goes. Even then I couldn't shake a queasy feeling that this was a dangerous trip for a U.S. president to be making on such short notice. We already knew that one of Córdoba's people was a Palo. There could be more. Then I noticed that on each side of us were two other choppers tagging along. We were over Los Pinos in a matter of minutes. Hovering over the open space in the garden-lawn, then slowly easing our way down. There was at least a company of Mexican special forces troops standing at alert and looking serious about what they were doing. President Córdoba was standing on the steps of the executive mansion, waiting.

The Secret Service guards got off first, then Dawson, then the rest of us, all trying to keep our hair from being blown off by the still-running chopper blades. I never have figured out why they don't just turn those things off. Dawson walked over to Córdoba and shook hands as though this was a routine campaign stop. Córdoba then turned to me and said, "Nice to see you again, professor. I hear you've had a busy day." I mumbled something back, wondering what he meant by that. Then we all followed our host down the corridor to the presidential office. We trooped in losing our entourage and Córdoba sat down at one end of the walnut conference table. Following his lead we all then sat down, Dawson next to Córdoba on one side, Moelker and I on the other. There was coffee and yellow pads and a closed file folder in front of Córdoba. He said, "Well, señores, what is to be done now?"

I decided to take the initiative since I was the one who missed the appointment with him yesterday. "Well, sir, I wanted to tell you I am sorry about not making our meeting yesterday, but I was unavoidably detained."

"So I understand, professor," he said. "You were kidnapped by Los Palos, and escaped only late last night. I'm pleased to see that you are all right. Los Palos were a dangerous group of *loco* fanatics."

"Excuse me, sir. But did you say 'were'?" I asked, looking over my glasses at Moelker, who just looked back. Dawson didn't say anything. I thought maybe Córdoba just got his "to be" verbs mixed up, which is easy enough for a native Spanish speaker to do. Then he opened the file folder on the table in front of him and began reading from some papers that looked like Telex. "Let's see, here. Our intelligence people and the army special forces raided a villa at Lake Pátzquaro at dawn this morning. Eight of Los Palos were killed. Three captured. There was a cache of arms, bombs, guns, terrorist equipment, and documents which detail their plan to overthrow this government . . . and a lot more."

This time I was feeling like Orphan Annie. We all just looked at each other. "You were lucky to get out when you did, professor," Córdoba said.

"So . . . ah . . . so, you knew I was there?" I said, now remembering Felipe's words on the plane—those who need to know will know.

"Yes, I've known since yesterday when you didn't show up for the meeting. I was . . . ah . . . advised about what happened. It does, I must say, put a new perspective on things."

"And Gómez-Hil?" I said. "You were informed about that, too?"

"Yes, but unfortunately Mr. Gómez-Hil is no longer with us. He had left before the raid but while driving back here through the mountains the brakes on his limousine failed. Both he and his driver are at the bottom of Mestizo Canyon. Those mountain roads are so very dangerous."

"Yes, that's too bad," I said. There was only one other question. "Sir, do you know if there was an American there?"

"That would be . . . let's see," Córdoba said, thumbing through his papers, "a . . . Mr. Halerpin? One of your CIA people who was apparently behind the whole thing?"

"Yes," I said, my heart pounding. "James Halerpin."

"There is no report on him here. He must have gotten out of there before the raid. But I suspect we'll catch up with him soon enough."

"We are . . ." Dawson said, "working on it."

"Yes, I would hope so," Córdoba said. And he smiled, poured himself a cup of coffee, leaned back in his chair, and said, "Well, gentlemen, I presume there is an agenda for this meeting?"

"Yes, indeed there is," Dawson said. "We have a proposal for you that I think will solve this debt problem."

"Okay, let's hear it." Córdoba said.

Dawson nodded to Moelker, who looked at me. I

looked back at him. Finally, Dawson said, "Mr. Moelker will present the details."

Moelker said, "Well, sir, here's what we would like to do. We would like to work with you to establish a joint Mexican-American debt adjustment agency. At first we will finance it by guaranteeing it a ten billion dollar loan. The agency will then issue bonds on the open market at, say, a five-to-one debt equity ratio. This will give it at least sixty billion operating capital.

"Then, initially, this agency—we would call it a Joint Development Finance Authority, or the JDFA—would exchange its bonds for the twenty billion debt of your state-owned enterprises that are now held by U.S. banks. Since the debt is now trading in the secondary market at far below market rates those bonds would also carry below-market rates. So the banks would give up some income but they would now have a safer investment. And, of course, they wouldn't have to write off the loans. So they would still be solvent."

"And the rest of the debt?" Córdoba said.

"As part of the agreement the banks will commit to loaning the agency, the JDFA, ten billion dollars over the next five years. These funds will then be used to purchase equity in the private Mexican corporations, that is, to exchange debt for equity and to finance direct investment into your private sector. This inflow of funds will essentially solve your balance of payments deficit. So far as the rest of the debt goes, most of it is, as you know, held by the IMF, the World Bank, and the IADB. They will put all loans to Mexico on long-term moratorium status. All interest due during that period will be paid by the U.S. government through capitalization of the Joint Development Finance Authority."

"Um-hum," Córdoba said, "and just what does 'long-term' moratorium mean?"

"Ten years," Moelker said, without hesitation, "then renegotiable for another ten if it seems necessary. I doubt that it will be, since by then oil prices should be back up."

"Let's make it twenty from the start," Córdoba said. Moelker looked at Dawson who looked like he was about to nod off.

Dawson said, "Okay, twenty it is."

The phone at Córdoba's side buzzed. "Bueno? Si . . . ah, si. Okay, muy bien," he said to someone. Then to us, he said, "The press people have somehow found out you're here. There are TV and newspaper people waiting out front. They want a statement from someone." I thought I saw a twinkle in his eye.

"Good," Dawson said, "that's good." He stood up and looked out at the presidential garden. "Let's get them out there on that lawn and tell them we have reached an agreement. Then I can get back to Washington and speak to the nation, and you can do the same here. That should settle it."

"All right, Mr. Dawson, we are in agreement," Córdoba said. "Let's have a joint communiqué drafted up. Then we can meet with the reporters." And he picked up the phone again and said something in rapid Spanish. An efficient-looking young Mexican popped into the room. Apparently his press secretary. "Mr. Sánchez will take care of the wording." Moelker, who I thought had been making notes handed Sánchez a couple of pages of scribbling.

He said, "Here it is." Sounding now like he was one of the most powerful men in the world, which he was. "Can you get us four copies of this to look over while you are doing the translation?"

Sánchez glanced at Córdoba, who nodded, and then said, "No problem," and scurried out of the room the way press secretaries do.

Through the picture window behind Córdoba's desk I could see a crowd of reporters gathering in the garden. TV cameras and a microphone being set up. Farther on, the three Marine helicopters looking totally incongruous. The crews were not in sight. Probably enjoying a game of poker inside, I couldn't help but reflect, as my mind began to wander from the proceedings at hand. Trivia. The rest was trivia. I had a "low tolerance for trivia," a dean had once told me. How to get out of here was the only thing I could think about. There were still some loose ends to tie up.

Heading south toward the airport far above Mexico City which was just a bowl of smog below us Dawson seemed to be his old self again. "Well, Cam," he said, "I guess this turned out to be a bit more than you bargained for. Why don't you come back with us on Air Force One? I think there is still a place for you in Washington. We could talk about it. Hammett's been wanting to go back to South Carolina. How would you like to take over Treasury?"

"Well, sir," I said, "that's interesting, but there are some details I've got to take care of here. I'll get back on my own. But thanks anyway. Treasury? That I'd like to think about."

"Look, Cam," Dawson said, "anything I can do for you, just let me know."

"Well, right now, if you could get this thing to take me back to the embassy, I would appreciate it."

"Consider it done, no problem." We were hovering

over the airport about to land next to Air Force One. When we did Dawson, Moelker, and the Secret Service agents got up to leave.

Moelker said, "It's been nice working with you again, professor. Let's keep in touch."

"I'd like that," I said.

Dawson had been talking to the pilot. "They'll take you back to the embassy, Cam. And, Cam . . . ah . . . thanks again." And he pumped my hand, the way presidents do.

As we took off again I could see him waving to a crowd of reporters, smiling as if everything was under control. I had a feeling of déjà vu, but it didn't last long. There were things to do, and time was of the essence. A few minutes of solitude for a change and we were hovering over the embassy roof easing in to land. Mitchell was there to meet me. After I cleared the wind tunnel he said, "The president said to do whatever we could to help you, professor. What can I do for you?"

"Just find me a private office with a phone," I said. "That's all I need." We walked quickly down the stairs and he ushered me into the same office I had used before. The legal attaché was still out of town it seemed. My little address book was somewhere with my clothes, so I dialed the embassy operator and said, "Get me Bill Anderson at Pearson, Fenway in Boston, please."

"Yes sir, right away."

In a couple of minutes the phone rang. "We have Mr. Anderson, sir," the operator said.

"Hi Bill. How's it been going?"

"Jeez, Cam, where have you been? I've been trying to get hold of you all day."

"I'm in Mexico City. Things have been a little hectic, as you may have noticed."

"Noticed? I've been awake for two days straight. Never saw anything like it. Everyone is going crazy. The market is closed and the . . ."

"I know, Bill, I know," I interrupted. "Look, what has happened to gold? Is the London exchange open?"

"Yes, and this morning's fix was eight-oh-five. You've made over a million dollars—on paper at least. That's why I was trying to get hold of you. What do you want to do?"

"Sell it all."

"Okay, whatever you say."

"And, Bill . . . take the million and deposit it in my checking account. Just put the rest back in the market. Okay?"

"Okay, consider it done."

"Thanks. I'll get back to you next week. Sorry, I've got to go." And I hung up. I hadn't had much time to think about whether that was illegal insider trading or not. It was, I decided, insider trading. But since all I knew at the time I bought the gold was that the president had said "My people tell me Mexico may default any day now." That wasn't any big news; it had been on the front page of the *Times* that same day. "Ah well," I said to myself, "that's something for the business ethics classes to discuss."

Without saying anything to Mitchell I walked out of the embassy on to the Paseo de la Reforma. The smog had cleared and the sun felt good. I headed toward the Geneve, looking for the clothing store on Londres that carries only British imports. It was still there. I bought a Harris Tweed sportcoat to replace the too-tight coat Lacy had found for me. "What's the exchange rate today?" I asked the impeccably dressed clerk.

"Nobody knows, señor," he said. "You'll have to charge it. We can't take cash."

I gave him my Preferred Citibank Visa, and said, "you can keep this one," handing him the coat I had been wearing. He just looked at me and shook his head. Mexicans have a certain stoicism when it comes to trying to understand Americans. They've given up asking questions.

Back in my suite at the Geneve I ordered up a ham and swiss sandwich and a double martini made with Tangueray. I ate it and drank it and then stood in the shower for a half an hour at least. Feeling was coming back to my arm and my head was shrinking back to its normal size. Then I laid down and took a nap. The banks were closed for siesta and wouldn't open again until four. Plenty of time for a nap. I needed it.

When I awoke it was almost five but it didn't matter. The banks would be open until seven. I ordered up another double martini and called Javier Neyra. Javier was the chief editor of Libros de Mexico and had edited a couple of my books that were published in Spanish. I trusted him and I knew he would know what I wanted to know.

"Hello, professor. How nice to see you." His English was terrible but he always wanted to practice on me. "You have news, I hope, otherwise you wouldn't be calling me from the States, no?"

"Hello, Javier. No, no news. I'm here in Mexico, and I need a favor. I need to ask you a favor."

"You are here? How wonderful. We'll have the dinner. Okay? Where are you?"

"Look, Javier, I'm in the Geneve but I don't have time for dinner. I just want to ask you *un pequeño favor*. I need some information."

"Okay, professor. I am your servant, as always. How can I do for you?"

"I need you to tell me the name of a reliable banker, here in Mexico City. I want to make a small investment. Who handles your company account?"

"A banquero? You want Enrique Lascano. He handles my accounts and he owes me many favors. He is quite trustworthy and very smart and ready, too. He is the manager of the Banamex. It's just two blocks around the block from you."

"Perfecto," I said. "Give him a call and tell him I'm coming to see him right away. Tell him it will be worth his time."

"Of course, professor, it's done. You want me to grease the road for you, is that it?"

"Yes, Javier, that's it, more or less."

"Good. Then we'll have the dinner. I want to tell you about your book. It's been selling like tortillas here."

"Sorry, Javier, I can't have dinner. I have to leave in the morning. But next time for sure. It's been good to talk to you."

"Well, equally to you professor. I'll call Enrique right now."

"Good. Thanks a lot, Javier. We'll see you. Nos Vemos."

XXIV

I walked around the corner and headed toward Insurgentes. "Just to your left," the desk clerk had said.

And the Banamex was there, looking imposing. Inside I told the receptionist who I was. She said, "Oh, yes, professor, the licenciado is expecting you." All lawyers in Mexico are "licensed" hence they are called licenciados. Everybody who is anybody is one. Only a few of them practice law. She led me to the back corner and into an ornate office which looked just as you would expect it to look.

"Professor Marshall! I'm so pleased to meet you," a plump balding, moustached man said as he jumped out from behind his desk. "Your reputation precedes you. Please sit down." In Mexico you have to pave the way ahead of yourself—or "grease the road" as Javier had perhaps more aptly put it—if you want to get anything done. I was glad I had called him. We exchanged fish handshakes, and I sat down in a leather covered overstuffed chair. "What can I do for you today?" he said.

"I want to set up a trust fund for someone," I said matter-of-factly.

"Well, of course, we'll be glad to handle that for you. What exactly do you have in mind?"

"I want to establish two funds and have the interest paid directly to two people I will designate. What rate are you paying now?"

"Right now? One hundred and twenty-five percent compounded annually if the money is put in certificates of deposit, which I would recommend, given everything that's been happening."

"Fine. Could you have the papers prepared now? I have to leave for the States in the morning."

"Yes, of course. And who will be the beneficiaries?" he asked, getting out some papers.

"One will be Señora José de Jesús Muñoz. The other Señora Arturo Octavio Cordes."

"Muñoz? José Muñoz was my cousin. It was so sad. We all miss him so very much. You can rest assured that I will handle this matter personally. And how much will you be putting into this worthy fund?"

"One million," I said, as I got out the check I always carry in my billfold and leaned over on his desk and began making it out.

"A million pesos. I'm sure that will be quite appreciated," he said. "That's very generous of you."

"One million dollars," I said, as I handed him the check. He looked up at me, started to say something. But apparently decided discretion was the better part of valor.

Finally, he said, "One million dollars. Divided equally between the two?"

"Yes."

I signed the papers and walked back toward the hotel. The restaurant that serves only prime rib was still on Hamburgo just around the corner. I had their largest and two martinis. Went back to the hotel and left a wake-up call for seven. And went to bed.

My plane left at nine, so I had breakfast, checked out and got into the nearest cab. "Good morning, boss" Felipe said.

"Hi, Felipe," I said, not surprised to see him. "Let's go to the airport."

"No problem, I'll have you there in a jiffy."

We negotiated the traffic while Felipe was telling me about the upcoming soccer games. At the terminal he hopped out opened the trunk and handed me my luggage and briefcase. "Where in the hell did you get those? I asked, pleased but not surprised.

"Oh, I don't know for sure, boss. They were just around someplace. Thought you might like to have them."

"Felipe," I said, "you take care of yourself, hear?"
"You too, boss." And he drove away.

I checked the luggage in, paid the departure tax and presented my ticket to the agent. "Let's see," she said. "You're a U.S. citizen, married . . . and your occupation?"

"University professor."